Choosing to Love

Gila Manolson

author of *The Magic Touch*, *Outside/Inside*, and *Head to Heart*

Choosing to Love

building a deep relationship with the right person — and with yourself

Distributed by
FELDHEIM PUBLISHERS
208 Airport Executive Park
Nanuet, NY 10954

P.O.B. 43163
Jerusalem, Israel

First Edition
July 2010

ISBN: 978-1-59826-611-5

Printed in Israel

Book Design by G. Kaye (02) 6519574

To Yehonatan

May you have as much love for the world
as we have for you

RABBI ZEV LEFF
Rabbi of Moshav Matityahu
Rosh Ḥayeshiva Yeshiva Gedola Matisyahu

הרב זאב לף
מרא דאתרא מושב מתתיהו
ראש הישיבה ישיבה גדולה מתתיהו

d.n. modiin 71917 ד.נ. מודיעין tel. 08-976-1138 טל׳ fax 08-976-5326 פקס

Chochmah is abstract knowledge, whereas *da'as* is the practical application of that knowledge. *Choosing to Love* adds to the *chochmah* of Mrs. Manolson's previous books — *The Magic Touch, Outside/Inside*, and *Head to Heart* — and also contributes a healthy dose of *da'as*: down-to-earth, real-life application.

The *chochmah* and *da'as* of *tznius* and relationships used to be learned at home, through intuition and osmosis. Today this requires an often impossible degree of insulation from the surrounding society. Consequently, many young adults — even those raised in a strong religious environment — are influenced by secular mores and attitudes. *Choosing to Love*, like all of Mrs. Manolson's books, is an invaluable source of healthy, Torah-based countervalues.

I commend Mrs. Manolson for her excellent, Torah-true presentation. May Hashem grant her and her family life, health, and prosperity, and may she continue benefitting the Jewish world.

With Torah blessings,

Zev Leff

Rabbi Zev Leff
Moshav Matityahu

בס"ד

NEVE · YERUSHALAYIM

נוה · ירושלים

Gila Manolson has done it again. Her finger is right on the pulse, and her sense of truth is right on target. In today's world, when confusion about love and identity abounds, her powerful message is more relevant than ever.

It is a great pleasure to know Gila and see her emerge as one of the Jewish world's most credible teachers and writers about relationships with others and with oneself.

Tziporah Heller

Tziporah Heller

Neve Yerushalayim

Contents

Preface 9
Acknowledgments 11
Introduction 13

Part 1: Loving Another 15
1: The Real Thing 19
2: Creating the Space for Love 39

Part 2: Loving Yourself 63
3: The Core Connection 67
4: Saying No to the Media 95
5: Ending the Hunger for Selfhood 109

Part 3: Getting There 121
6: Building Love 123

Final Words 143
Conclusion 155

Notes 157
References 171
About the Author 179

Preface

For a long time, I've wanted to write another book, one that would really make a difference. I wanted a topic no one had written about — something totally new. The question was, what?

Meanwhile, everywhere I went, teenagers and adults alike weren't asking for anything new. They couldn't get enough of the practically bottomless topics of love, *tzniut* (modesty), and being *shomer negiah* (not touching the opposite sex before marriage).

Still I persisted: Surely one of my passions could translate into an exciting new bestseller. Maybe Judaism and the environment? Judaism and healthy eating? Judaism and exercise? Judaism and crocheting? (All right, crocheting isn't a passion, but I was getting desperate.)

I was about to give up, when finally it dawned on me: I don't need a new topic. I need to speak more broadly and deeply about what I've always spoken about — what people still want and need to hear.

Choosing to Love is a sequel to my previous books, *The Magic Touch: A Jewish Approach to Relationships, Outside/ Inside: A Fresh Look at Tzniut*, and *Head to Heart: What to Know before Dating and Marriage.* I recommend that you read them first, as they discuss many important issues not repeated here. Yet even if you start with *Choosing to Love*, you'll find its insights crucial for our times.

A famous woman once wrote: "We teach what we need to learn and write what we need to know." In sharing my thoughts with others, I clarify them for myself. After writing *Choosing to Love*, I believe more than ever in its message. After reading it, I hope the ideas in this book will change your life as they've changed mine.

Acknowledgments

I have no words to thank Hashem for blessing me with such a deeply fulfilling life and for making so many wonderful people part of it.

As always, I'm indebted to Rabbi Zev Leff, without whose backing I would never have had the courage to publish my first book, and who has remained a pillar of support; and to Rebbetzin Tziporah Heller, whose understanding of *tzniut* has guided virtually everything I do and whose teachings have become an integral part of my consciousness.

I'm tremendously grateful to many special people (listed here in alphabetical order) for their input on the manuscript: psychologist Rebecca Drill, for her positive energy and invaluable comments (despite her ideological differences with Orthodox Judaism); psychologist and teacher Yocheved (Jackie) Engel, for her spiritual perspective on self-worth and much more; Sara Batya Friedman, soul sister, for her fine-tuned sensitivity and insight and for emphasizing the need for Chapter 6; Marina Goodman, loyal friend and author of *"Why Should I Stand behind the Mechitzah When I Could Be a Prayer Leader?"*, for her incisive comments and unflagging support; my sister Joanne Lang, master of "shades of gray," for challenging me and forcing me to be honest; Erika (Levin) Needleman, outstanding student of life, for her beyond-her-years wisdom; Jeremy Rovinsky, a great Shabbat guest, for not letting engagement, marriage, and law school prevent him from offering assistance; my sister Ellen Rozics, for her down-to-earth combination of depth and practicality; Leah Schachter, my hostess *par excellence*, for keeping my writing "real" and reader-friendly; Simone Skopek, long-lost friend, for her uncommon sense and intelligence; Tzipporah Stein, for her heartwarming enthusiasm; and Yael Tzvia (Julia) Weiss-Schwalb, my "sunshine," for her gentle, on-the-mark suggestions. (It was hard to pinpoint what to thank each person for — what I wrote for one could easily be said for others as well.)

I'm also grateful to the following busy people who reviewed or helped with parts of the book: Paula Mack Drill, Yehonasan Gefen, Auriel Manolson, Chanie Micahnek, Sara Yocheved Rigler, Tova Saul, Tzippi Schechet (Shaked), Arkady Shraybman, Shlomo Simkins, Yehudit Meira (Yomaira) Tamayo, and Chaya Riva Tarnapolsky.

My heartfelt thanks to Esther Malka Fein for getting the creative juices going, resulting in a title.

A special thanks to Rabbi Yitzchak Feldheim for his interest and delicate revision.

Most of all, I thank my wonderful husband, Avraham, not only for his discernment and clarity, but for his constant love and belief in me. My apologies to him and to our precious children, Chananya and Daniella, Elyashiv, Yair, Temima, Emuna, Ayelet, and Yisrael, who received less attention while I was writing. I hope they feel the result was worth it.

Introduction

I grew up in a society that extolled both love between a man and a woman and self-love, yet was often capable of neither. "What the world needs now is love, sweet love / It's the only thing that there's just too little of," the radio sang to us — while the divorce and teenage suicide rates soared. Sentiments about love can fly high, but without knowing how to realize them, they're not worth much.

This book is about two kinds of love: for oneself, and for another. Both are essential to a deeply satisfying life. And the two are inextricable: Our relationships with others can be only as healthy and deep as our relationship with ourselves; at the same time, it can be easier to love ourselves when we know someone special does too. We must understand and learn how to develop both kinds of love.

Yet so many forces work against us. Advertising worms its way into every corner of our globalized world, selling the illusion that our deepest pleasure lies in products, not people.

Our fast-paced, electronic life propels us toward immediate gratification, rather than relationships developed over time. And in an increasingly superficial society, we falsely define our bodies as ourselves and equate physical attraction with love.

Thankfully, we're not hopeless — we just need wisdom. The best source, ideally, is the home. Unfortunately, we don't necessarily get it there. Nor do we learn it at school. Public high schools prepare us primarily for university, and universities prepare us primarily to enter the work force. We end up knowing more about how to make a living than how to live. Rarely if ever are courses offered in "Education for Life," "Love," and "Personal Growth and Self-Discovery."

So we have to seek wisdom ourselves. Seminaries and yeshivahs for *ba'alei teshuvah* (those who've "returned" to Jewish observance) often provide it in abundance. My husband and I have hosted innumerable students from such schools at our Shabbat table. Many, if not most, come from broken homes — yet most end up happily married. It's also immensely gratifying to see these young women and men blossom into self-aware, internally defined, and deeply developed individuals. All these people realized what they were missing, sought wisdom, integrated it into their lives, and benefit from it to this day. They recognized that, as one author put it, "the life of the soul is at stake in human relationships" — including our relationships with ourselves — and they committed themselves to "getting it right." They learned to love.

This book, like my others, is intended to contribute to this education. May *Choosing to Love* help you forge a meaningful and rewarding relationship with yourself and with another.*

---

* While the stories included herein are true, names are fictitious.

PART ONE
LOVING ANOTHER

Judging by popular music, nothing is more sought after than love. Yet true love eludes many, and often for good reason: Either we don't know what love is, or we don't know how to get it.

Before you can love someone, you must love yourself. Healthy self-love is a prerequisite for a healthy relationship. Without this key ingredient, you may subconsciously want your partner to be everything you believe you aren't, resulting in unrealizable expectations and unnecessary disappointment. At the same time, it may be hard to believe someone genuinely loves you when you yourself don't.

Unfortunately, self-love doesn't always come easily. Outer and inner beauty can be more apparent in others than in ourselves. Furthermore, learning to love ourselves may entail changing our self-image — which can be challenging, if not downright scary. For these reasons, this book speaks first about loving another, then about the more difficult topic of loving oneself.

Part 1 is about attaining male-female love. Chapter 1, "The Real Thing," is a continuation of *Head to Heart: What to Know before Dating and Marriage* (primarily the fourth chapter), offering more ideas about how to begin a beautiful relationship with the right person. Chapter 2, "Creating the Space for Love," picks up where *The Magic Touch: A Jewish Approach to Relationships* left off, describing the workings of the most amazing tool for attaining that relationship: being *shomer negiah* — observing the laws of touch, which prohibit physical contact with the opposite sex before marriage.* These chapters will guide you toward healthy, lifelong love.

* I heartily recommend reading *Head to Heart* and *The Magic Touch* before reading Chapters 1 and 2, although each chapter briefly reviews the relevant book's central theme.

1

The Real Thing

After more than enough dating, it was clear: Avraham, today my husband, was going to propose. But first, he told me, protocol required that I meet the head of his yeshivah.

Avraham led me into the *rosh yeshivah*'s office. An imposing, decidedly rabbinic-looking figure sat behind a large desk. "So this must be Gila," he said with a warm smile, immediately putting me at ease. He and Avraham exchanged a few pleasantries, and then my soon-to-be-fiancé politely exited.

Still smiling, the rabbi asked me a bit about myself. The conversation flowed, and I was certain I was making a great impression.

Then there was a pause. The *rosh yeshivah* leaned forward in his chair and gazed at me intently. "So," he said, "give me a definition of love."

Uh-oh — I wasn't prepared for this kind of question. But I'd done so well so far, I figured I could handle it. "Love,"

I began confidently, "is that feeling you have...when you feel...that you have that — feeling..." I trailed off, my self-assurance dissipating.

That's when it hit me: I'm expecting to love my husband-to-be — in fact, I think I'm already starting to — but I can't even define love.

What Is Love?*

"Love" is probably the most misunderstood word in the world. One popular, purportedly profound notion is that love is too mysterious and elusive to explain logically. "Love cannot be defined," expounds a New Age magazine. "One cannot learn to love, for love is found beyond learning. All one can do is remove the obstacles. Love is found in the singular realm of experience." In my humble opinion, this is nonsense — and depressing as well, for if love can't be defined, you can't actively pursue it. Having removed the obstacles, you simply sit back and hope you'll be one of those fortunate people in whose "singular realm of experience" love magically appears. If you're not, tough luck.

Others, however — like me on the eve of my engagement — will valiantly attempt to define love, often coming up with: "Love is that feeling you get when you meet the right person." But this definition is dangerously mistaken.

First, love is more than a feeling. It has to be, for feelings alone can't establish a lasting bond. While physical attraction, chemistry, and connection are essential and add excitement to a loving relationship, they can also unconsciously draw you to a lousy human being, a grown-up baby, an

* For a fuller discussion, see *Head to Heart.*

abuser, or someone just totally wrong for you. And even if being with that person feels good, feelings are fickle; they can be here today, gone tomorrow.

Therefore, while love entails and culminates in intense emotion, it must be based on something more solid: reason. Preferably *before* losing your head, you must delve deeply into who the other is, evaluating not only his or her personality but, more importantly, his or her *character* and *values*. You must identify his or her virtues, and they must be rooted in a belief system strong enough to withstand temptation. Whether your date is liberal or conservative, deliberate or spontaneous, or extroverted or introverted may be important, but these labels will impact your relationship less than whether he or she is caring, loyal, patient, responsible, honest, willing to work things out, and morally unshakeable. The same is true for you: Love is not about just finding the right person but *being* the right person. If you don't possess the values and character you'd want the other to have, get to work.

In addition to seeing the good in each other, love requires that you remain focused on it. It's your choice whether to magnify your partner's worst or best qualities, and because emotions often stem from thoughts, what you think significantly affects what you feel.

In short: Love is a discipline. It requires not only your heart but your head.

If love isn't just a feeling, we needn't wait to for it to happen. We can *make* it happen. As one author succinctly put it: "Love is a verb." Love stems from acting lovingly. In expressing care, respect, affection, and appreciation for the other — and, more than anything else, giving unconditionally — *we create love.* We may not want to admit it, but rather than some mystical force, "bigger than both of us," love is something we choose.

Love, then, is not only emotional — it's also rational; not passive, but highly active. I would therefore define it much as my husband's *rosh yeshivah* did: *Love is the emotional attachment that results from deeply appreciating, in thought and deed, another's goodness.* Or, in the words of a well-known psychologist: "Love is not just feeling and passion. Love is a system of attitudes and a series of acts which engender growth and enhance life for both lover and beloved." And those attitudes and acts come from being moved by goodness.

A husband and wife with this kind of love won't throw in the towel when their relationship takes a downturn. Instead, they'll say: "Underneath it all, you're still that same good person you've always been. So if some of the good feelings have gone, we'll have to get them back — because the basis of this relationship is still solid." This is the love that lasts.

Looking for What Matters

So love means appreciating another's goodness. But isn't it important to have the same interests? Such compatibility definitely helps launch and maintain a relationship — but it can't be the basis of lifelong love. For one thing, interests can change. More important, they distract us from the real glue of a relationship.

I once met the perfect couple. Larry and Linda were on the same page in virtually everything: travel, politics, diet, the environment, you name it. I had never seen two people so made for one another. And they seemed so happy together. It was enviable.

They're now divorced.

Despite their amazing compatibility, why didn't it last? Neither Larry nor Linda possessed the ethic of striving to improve themselves. Nor did they see marriage as a spiritual path, a sacred bond to commit to and work on. As a result, self-centeredness took over, leaving each one more devoted to himself/herself than to the other or to their crumbling relationship.

To succeed in love, we must focus on what matters most — character and values, including the ethos of self-improvement and commitment to the relationship. Unfortunately, you won't learn this formula from the media. Imagine a women's magazine whose cover proclaims: "Shed Those Bad *Middot* [character traits] before the Summer!" "Selfish Binges: Kick the Habit Today," and "Drive a Man Crazy with Your Morality!" Character doesn't sell. So if we don't want to be sold garbage instead, we have to develop a healthy skepticism about what we're bombarded with.

Advertising is a good place to begin. Take an ad that appeared in *Yale Alumni Magazine*, targeting a purportedly highly intelligent audience: It featured a good-looking, well-coiffed, smartly dressed man wearing an expensive watch (being advertised), sitting confidently by the Jacuzzi in his penthouse apartment overlooking Los Angeles. The copy read: "Daniel Bernhardt, Hollywood. Doesn't need a life coach."

Really? Is life just about financial success? Does this rich, fashionable, self-assured guy have what it takes to genuinely love a woman? If not, a life coach might be just what he needs.

Personal ads are also a great tool for honing one's critical faculties. Here's a typical, upscale one: "Passionate Artist; lovely, thoughtful, successful painter. Naturally slender, athletic, divorced, good-looking with mischievous spark. Enjoys ideas, morning walks, photography, books, DVDs, cross-country skiing, planning dinners with interesting mixes of friends. Loves ease, conviviality of eating out — intimate conversation across the table, someone else to cook and do dishes. Lives wonderful life, just missing someone special — friendly, fit, active, New England area man, 58 to 73."

While this lady certainly sounds interesting, is she a good person? What if, like some passionate artists, she's moody and self-absorbed? What if she uses those dinners with interesting mixes of friends to gossip? What if loving having someone else cook and do dishes means she's selfish and lazy? And how about the man she's seeking? He could be a friendly, fit, active, New England area, sixty-five-year-old axe murderer. (Or, to be more realistic, a deadbeat dad with no connection to his children from two previous marriages, both of which terminated due to his unfaithfulness.)

While many personal ads disregard character and values in favor of interests and personality, others stoop even lower. My friend Andrea saw one in *Philadelphia Magazine*: "Jewish Prince Looking for Needle in Haystack. Successful international businessman, 35, seeking beautiful, highly educated woman, 22–29. Her measurements must be . . . PHOTO A MUST."

Andrea couldn't resist responding to the ad: "I have just the woman. She's 25, stunning, and brilliant. But her measurements aren't exactly what you specified. Interested?"

The "prince" replied: "Possibly — BUT YOU MUST SEND A PHOTO!"

She wrote back: "Glad to know you're flexible. The woman in question, however, informed me that she feels a man who specifies a woman's measurements as opposed to her character probably isn't deep or spiritually developed enough to maintain a loving relationship."

It's All About — Whom?

The fact that love means appreciating another's goodness implies something equally fundamental: Love means going beyond oneself.

Love is based on true appreciation of the other. Girls frequently ask me: "When a guy says 'I love you,' how do I know he means it?" I have a standard reply: "Ask him what he loves about you, and then ask yourself if that's who you are."

My young friend Amy asked her intelligent, articulate boyfriend why he loves her, expecting a deep and moving reply. He responded affectionately, "Because you're so cute."

"Because I'm so *cute*?!" she retorted. "Then why don't you get a puppy?"

After breaking up with him, Amy told me, "My ex-boyfriend saw me primarily as an ornament. He wasn't interested in really knowing me."

Not only wasn't this love that could last, it wasn't love to begin with.

People also sometimes ask me if I believe in love at first sight. Attraction at first sight, definitely. Sensing the possibility of a real connection at first sight, sure. But if love stems from knowledge, "love at first sight" is a contradiction in terms. You can't know someone at first sight.

In addition to genuinely knowing the other, love requires that your emotions center on him or her. I once saw a magazine photo of some Hollywood-type guy and the former model he was seeing. The caption, quoting him, read: "I'm in love with love!"

What in the world does that mean?

Picture yourself as a woman standing in the moonlight with the man of your dreams. There's a long silence as you gaze adoringly at each other. Then he stammers, "I...I just have to tell you…"

At long last — the moment you've been waiting for. "Yes?" you answer breathlessly.

"I want you to know...I...I…" Overcome with emotion, he can barely get the words out.

"Yes? Yes?" You feel dizzy. It's coming — what you've been longing to hear.

He takes a deep breath and looks lovingly into your eyes. "I'm so in love with — *love*."

Would you find that gratifying? I doubt it. He's not in love with *you* — he's in love with a feeling, and this romance has conveniently provided it. This is all about him. You? You're interchangeable.

When I was in eleventh grade (and not yet religious), a twelfth-grader who didn't know me at all asked me out. I was surprised, but I said okay. "Do want to go horseback riding?" he asked eagerly.

I don't know where he got the idea that I was a horsewoman. "To tell you the truth, I'm scared of horses," I confessed. His face fell. "Oh," he said. With far less excitement, he tried to think of something else we could do, and we ended up going bowling.

Now, this boy may just have really liked horseback riding, thought it would be fun to do together, and was disappointed when I didn't share his enthusiasm. But I can't help feeling it wasn't necessarily me he was interested in. He dreamed of galloping across a field with some girl, her hair blowing in the wind — but it didn't have to be me or my hair. I was just someone he could plug into his fantasy. He wanted to be in love with love.

This pursuit of self-centered "love" fits our self-centered society. If life is essentially about me, then love needn't be anything more than a way for me to get my needs and desires fulfilled. True love, however, is other-oriented: It means often putting someone else first.

A teenager told me about her friend Shani's struggle. Shani's boyfriend had decided (wisely, I thought) that rather than investing in a relationship at this time in his life, he needed to be studying to secure his future. He suggested they stop seeing each other for now. Shani was fighting the idea.

"Does Shani love her boyfriend?" I asked.

"Of course — that's why she can't bear the idea of no longer seeing him," my young acquaintance replied sadly.

"I'm sure this is very hard for her," I sympathized. "But trying to change his mind means Shani loves herself more than him. If her feelings for him are genuine, she won't want to keep him from doing what he has to do — as painful for her as it may be." True love means caring about another person's needs and desires as much, or more, as you care about your own.* As

* Obviously, in a mutually satisfying relationship, this attitude is reciprocal.

a famous woman said: In romantic love, you want the other person; in real love, you want what's best for the other person.

The "In Love" Phenomenon

So being "in love with love" won't lead to a true relationship. Does that mean being "in love" with another person will? As thrilling as this experience is, not necessarily. Many if not most relationships entail being "in love," and most — including most marriages — end.

The problem with being "in love" is that you don't see the other clearly. In the words of one relationship expert, people in love "engage in a full-blown idealization of the other....[they] have blocked out reality." Scientific research backs this up. Listen to an authority in the field: "Falling in love is one of the most irrational behaviors or brain states imaginable for both men and women. The brain becomes 'illogical' in the throes of new romance, literally blind to the shortcomings of the lover.... [This documented brain state] shares brain circuits with states of obsession, mania, intoxication, thirst, and hunger.... The brain circuits that are activated when we are in love match those of the drug addict desperately craving the next fix."

So by all means, be madly, passionately, blindly in love — *after* verifying that the other person is genuinely wonderful. Otherwise, this "love" will eventually die, because this overcharged brain state* usually lasts no longer than a year or two, and then illusions give way to reality. Real love

* Characterized by elevated levels of dopamine, a hormone associated with reward-seeking — the reward in this case being love (Kuchinskas, *The Chemistry of Connection*, 78).

requires a clear, calm vision of the other's qualities — including acceptance of faults. Only a relationship based not just on attraction but on appreciation of the other's goodness will survive the "in love" stage and metamorphose into a long-term attachment. Such a relationship involves a completely different brain state, in which excitement — while by no means absent — makes room for more sustainable and ultimately more profound feelings of connection. When romance is coupled with a peaceful sense of ever-growing closeness, love deepens and endures.

Don't Categorize — Experience

While objectivity is essential in dating, this doesn't mean viewing others coldly from the outside. On the contrary, really knowing someone means seeing him or her from the inside. A woman told me about a rabbi who spoke in her community. "When you meet new people," he advised, "instead of judging them, take them in as they are. Don't categorize them — *experience* them."

Most of us relate to people somewhat superficially. We size them up quickly and shallowly, concluding — based on preconceptions — that we've "got their number." This tendency is common in dating, especially among those suffering from dating burn-out. Upon meeting someone new, we immediately decide we know enough about the person to know he or she is not for us. We dismiss people before ever really seeing them.

I once spoke about love at a singles' gathering. There was lots of good food and music — and naturally, everyone was discreetly looking around, hoping to meet somebody. I too looked around, grateful to be happily married and feeling for all these people yearning to find the "right one." I wondered what it would be like to be single at an event like this. Would I be hopeful or pessimistic?

I wasn't sure. On the one hand, all the participants seemed nice. On the other hand, some were more attractive or successful than others. Would I, like numerous singles, gravitate only toward the former? And upon realizing that, for whatever reason, they wouldn't be interested in me, would I simply write off the evening as a depressing waste of time?

Or could I look at these "others" differently?

I decided to experiment: If someone wanted to talk to me after my lecture, I would try to transcend superficial impressions. I would try to see him or her in a real way. Rather than categorize, I would experience.

Several people indeed approached me. All asked intelligent, sensitive questions about the true meaning of love and how to achieve it. None had the looks or charisma of a Hollywood celebrity. One even suffered from a serious degenerative disease. Yet everyone came through loud and clear as a beautiful human being. Suddenly the room seemed full of unbelievably eligible singles. I felt like calling out, "Hey, everyone! Do you know what a gold mine we have here?! Make sure you meet this one, and this one, and this one!"

Much has been written and spoken about the dating crisis. So many wonderful singles just can't find that "right one." There are undoubtedly a host of reasons for this tragic state of affairs, many of which have to do with societal problems rather than individual shortcomings. I don't want to point a finger at those who may already have come under attack for being "too picky." Yet I can't help but wonder: Could part of the problem be that we simply don't see people deeply and uniquely? Because we categorize rather than experience?

Next time you're on a date or at a singles' event, try the experiment. Drop your preconceptions. Open your mind and heart, and let the other person in. He or she may prove a lot more attractive than you expect. Maybe even beautiful.

Preserving Subjectivity

Once you've objectively decided whom you want to spend your life with, it's time for utter *subjectivity.* Comparisons to others become irrelevant, for when you look at your beloved, you love what you see. The idealization that's so dangerous when you're "in love" is a boon once you're married to Mr. or Ms. Right.

Yet subjectivity is becoming increasingly unattainable — particularly in the physical realm. In revealing everything, the media have replaced subjectivity with cold objectivity. Today, every inch of a person's face or body is crassly scrutinized and measured against other people's — or worse, against artificial images. In the end, a human being is reduced to a mere specimen, an object.

This destruction of subjectivity is a death sentence for love. Research has found that young single men who even briefly viewed stereotypically beautiful women on TV or in men's magazines were more critical of other women's looks than were men unexposed to these images. Far worse, married men shown photos of such women, as opposed to those shown pictures of average-looking women, found their wives less attractive and felt less committed to their marriages. And another group of married men who looked at revealing photos of models later described themselves as less in love with their wives.

Though less visually oriented than men, women too have been affected by the assault on subjectivity. From the 1930s, when mass media debuted, to the 1990s, men's desire to marry a "good-looking" woman increased by 40%, while women's desire to marry a "good-looking" man increased by 80% (and "good-looking" inevitably invokes an objective, media-promulgated standard). By 1996, a good-looking spouse was more important to women than it had been to men in 1939.

No wonder everyone's biggest fear (particularly women's) is that natural enemy of beauty: aging. But if we embrace subjectivity, aging needn't be so frightening. There's a beautiful and poignant scene in *The Five People You Meet in Heaven* by Mitch Albom. Eighty-three-year-old Eddie, a widower for over three decades, is killed in a tragic accident. In heaven, he reunites with his wife, Marguerite. In their lifetime, they had a deeply loving marriage, and as they had no children, she was everything to him — until she died of cancer. And here she is in heaven, young and beautiful once again.

Their reunion is moving:

> "Can I ask you something?" he said.
>
> "Yes."
>
> "How come you look the way you looked the day I married you?"
>
> "I thought you'd like it that way."
>
> He thought for a moment. "Can you change it?"
>
> "Change it?" She looked amused. "To what?"
>
> "To the end."
>
> ..."I wasn't so pretty at the end."
>
> Eddie shook his head, as if to say not true.
>
> "Could you?"

In the movie version of the book, Marguerite's back is to you, and as they turn, you recoil in shock — for she has suddenly become a sickly, middle-aged woman. Her eyes are lined with little wrinkles, her hair is thinning and half-gray, and the skin beneath her chin is loose. But as she gazes up at her husband, you cease comparing her to her younger self, or to anyone else. For twenty-plus years of love pour forth from this forty-seven-year-old woman's eyes. And you begin seeing her as Eddie does — he gazes back at her lovingly with a look that says, "You're as beautiful as ever."

We're born subjective. Young children rarely compare their mothers' looks to other women's — they just love their mothers. But subjectivity must be protected and nurtured. We have to shield ourselves from destructive media images, while strengthening our consciousness of every person's beauty. The more successful we are, the more we can love.

Staying Grounded

As valuable as subjectivity is, it's important to keep your feet on the ground. True, Judaism believes every match is made in Heaven, but invoking Heaven can inspire quite a bit of romantic fantasy. Unfortunately, many observant young adults graft the media's false notions of love onto the Jewish concept of a "soul mate." The resulting ideal is a kind of secular-religious hybrid, in which the dashing Torah scholar and his glamorous wife-to-be "fall in love" on their first date. This vision is bound to disappoint, for disappointment arises from a discrepancy between expectations and reality — and if our expectations stem from movies and romance novels, the discrepancy will be great.

I believe in living in reality. That's why I never understood what could be so great about recreational drugs: A mind-altering substance makes you feel good for a while — but then it wears off, and you're back in the real world. So why not look for life's greatest pleasures in the real world to begin with?

Anything that removes you from reality for too long lessens your ability to appreciate it. No matter how high you're flying in a relationship, everyone eventually comes down to earth after the honeymoon (or *sheva brachot**). This landing is normal and nothing to fear. But some hit the ground hard, leaving themselves badly bruised. Others touch down more lightly and easily. It all depends whether you've envisioned your soul mate as a fantasy or as a real person.

Seeing your partner in real terms means recognizing that the two of you won't be perfectly compatible, nor will he or she meet all your emotional needs. There is no such thing as a perfect match. *A soul mate is someone to grow with.* God wants to give us pleasure, and therefore, just as food usually tastes good, being with one's soul mate usually feels good. And when it does, the recognition of what a blessing he or she is largely outshines minor disappointments.

Sometimes, however, being with your soul mate doesn't feel good. Then it takes real spiritual greatness to recognize that, like everything else, this person was brought into your life for a reason.

I know a woman with this greatness. Her marriage isn't easy, and some may conclude that she simply chose the wrong person. But she recognizes that her relationship with

* The six days of festive meals following the wedding.

her husband has caused her to grow in ways she never would have otherwise — and if life is about growth, then maybe he is indeed her soul mate.

While we all want growth, no one wants it through difficulty and pain (and sometimes divorce is necessary). Yet a spiritual perspective on the concept of a "soul mate" gives us the strength and courage to face challenges, thereby becoming greater human beings.

Hopefully, though, if we approach love with the preparation and thoughtfulness it deserves,* our soul mate will bring us more joy than anything else.

To Become One

One of the great joys of marriage is knowing that the other person isn't leaving. College-age Tammi once shared the following painful situation with me. "I loved my boyfriend, and I thought he loved me," she said sadly, "but now it's over. It wasn't supposed to end this way. I thought we'd be together for — " she stopped, as if catching herself, "um, for a really long time."

Something sounded wrong. "You wanted to say 'for*ever*,' didn't you?" I asked.

Tammi hesitated, then nodded.

"But you didn't, because it's not cool to believe in 'forever' anymore, right?"

She was silent.

Judaism believes in forever. We're interested not in temporary good feelings, but in love that lasts a lifetime. This eternal bond — marriage — requires that we strive for

---

* Including counseling, if necessary.

something that independent-minded individuals often find very difficult: oneness.

We can learn a lot about oneness from the conjoined twins Abigail and Brittany Hensel. Born in 1990, these girls developed from an egg that didn't completely separate, resulting in what's called dicephalus twins. They're two people, each with her own head and organs above the waist; yet their torsos are fused, and below the waist, their body narrows into that of one person. They share two arms and legs, with each girl controlling her side of their body, meaning that an activity as simple as walking requires intricate coordination. Yet they've developed such a high level of cooperation that they type, swim, play sports, and even drive. On the other hand, if they're running and one suddenly stops, both fall. Anything either does affects them both, for they're physically one.

Unlike the Hensel twins, a man and woman are two separate beings. Their union isn't imposed upon them by biology, but is freely chosen. At the same time, like the Hensel twins, they're a unit, and whatever either does affects them both. When husband and wife coordinate all their efforts and prioritize their relationship, they're successful and happy — for spiritually, they're one.

Spiritual oneness, rooted in independent free will, requires that each person first be autonomous. In mature love, each person belongs to himself/herself and is free to become his or her best self. Before you can have a healthy relationship, you must know who you are and be able to live happily and productively on your own.

This "autonomy within oneness" characterized the sixty-year marriage of Rabbi Simcha and Rebbetzin Feiga Rochel Wasserman, both of blessed memory. Having no children, they were each other's world — and when I visited their home years ago, their love was palpable. Yet they were very much two free-standing individuals. Decades earlier, Rabbi Wasserman's commitment to Jewish education had taken him far from home, and for nearly two years, the couple had lived apart, with the rebbetzin investing most of her earnings in her husband's work. After he died and she finished sitting *shivah** for him, she remarked, "I thought I couldn't live without him, but you see, I can." She could — but nevertheless, a few hours after completing her last kindness for her husband, she too left this world. She wasn't afraid of being alone. Rather, her soul simply longed to be with his.

Life has many blessings, but we don't always appreciate them. My family and I live nearly at the peak of our mountaintop neighborhood. "Wow! You have an incredible view!" our guests exclaim. We do — but I've become used to it. I take it for granted.

Over time, it can be hard not to take love for granted. Instead of appreciating it, we become critical and fault-finding: "But she's lacking this," we grumble; or "If only he had that." We can lose the gratitude we once felt for this special person.

We have to work hard to prevent that — and we can start gearing ourselves up while we're still single. The most joyful, radiant people are those who are grateful for every little thing. *Love is huge.* If we let it, the recognition that we're loved and have someone to love can fill our hearts to overflowing every day. As one married person writes: "God's greatest gift, after

* The seven-day period of mourning.

life itself, is love. God created [your spouse] for you. Love your husband with all your heart and treat him like the gift from God that he is." If we develop this appreciation for our soul mate before we've even found him or her, we'll be more likely to love that person forever.*

Nearly everyone dreams of true love. Making that dream come true requires not only a solid character and healthy values, but also the right approach to dating. And within that approach, one practical tool stands out: Being *shomer negiah*.

* For more on having a successful relationship, I highly recommend Chana Levitan's wise and practical guide, *I Only Want to Get Married Once: Dating Secrets for Getting It Right the First Time* (Jerusalem: Gefen Publishing House, 2010).

2
Creating the Space for Love

I once addressed a group of secular high school students about relationships in Judaism, including the benefits of being *shomer negiah*. Afterward, a sixteen-year-old approached me. "What you said got me thinking," he admitted. "If we took physicality out of the picture, my girlfriend and I wouldn't have much going."

So many "relationships" aren't what they should be — and the emotional cost can be great. (While this guy's realization didn't devastate him, what about his girlfriend?) Still, people find it hard to break from our society's norms of casual male-female interaction — and being *shomer negiah* is a radical departure. But nothing less will rectify the situation we've gotten ourselves into.

Why Be *Shomer Negiah*?*

Jewish mysticism teaches that Adam and Eve were originally joined together, separated only later. Deep down, in the recesses of our minds, we "remember" once having been one with someone of the opposite sex; and now that we're separate and alone, we yearn to regain that original oneness. Humans long for connection.** And we seek relationships that will satisfy this profound emotional need.

But they often don't. Too commonly, we *feel* close but we actually *aren't* close. Being close is what our souls crave. It requires a deep investment of self; it takes time; and it lasts. Feeling close is just that — a feeling. It can be short-lived. And it requires very little. Sometimes all it takes is a touch.

Touch bonds — especially for women. It breaks down walls, leaving us feeling warm and open toward the other. We may not even know him or her, but pleasurable physical contact makes us feel close. This is so even if the touch is merely friendly — and immeasurably more so if it's romantic.

This illusory bond destroys your objectivity. You see only what you want to see. How could that guy whose touch makes my head spin be cruel? How could that girl who makes me feel so wonderful be selfish? With this skewed vision, you may later find yourself engaged or even married to someone who proves to be quite different from the person you thought you knew. Without the illusion of emotional

---

* For a fuller discussion of these and many other ideas — including the price of experience, gender differences, the value of innocence, and platonic relationships — see *The Magic Touch*.

** Females in particular are guided by what has been called the "intimacy imperative." (Gurian, *The Wonder of Girls*, 23.)

closeness, we can evaluate and appreciate each other's genuine worth. Not getting physical while dating, difficult as it may be, helps preserve clarity and prevents us from making tragic mistakes.

Perhaps the saddest mistake of all concerns the powerful word "love." True love focuses solely on the other. Too often, however, "love" is self-oriented. No matter how sincerely a man tells a woman (or a woman tells a man), "I love you," he may not realize he's really saying, "I love the way you make *me* feel." He doesn't love *her*; he loves what she does to *him*. This isn't love — it's narcissism. When two people in a relationship aren't giving each other physical pleasure, it's much easier for them to appreciate the other solely for who he or she really is. Refraining from touch creates the space in which true love can develop.

Finally, being *shomer negiah* revives a nearly defunct concept: specialness. "*Shomer*," usually translated as "keeping" or "guarding," also means "cherishing." *Judaism wants us to cherish touch.* Touch should be meaningful. Life isn't about how much you do with how many people; it's about the depth of what you share with one special person. Instead of diluting the power of physicality by spreading it thin (and accumulating a lot of unwanted memories), being *shomer negiah* concentrates it into what can bring you the most satisfaction and joy: your lifelong relationship.

Everyone wants genuine closeness, but there are no short-cuts — and getting physical won't get you there at all. Judaism advises: Leave physicality on the side for now. Build a connection that's heart-to-heart, not just skin-to-skin. Once you're married to the right person, physicality can enter the picture. Then, instead of creating artificial closeness, touch will express a true spiritual connection.

Being *shomer negiah* is challenging, but it's no less a part of Jewish law than Shabbat — and no less a gift from God, for its spiritual benefits are immense. As we'll see, being *shomer negiah* greatly increases your chance of avoiding pitfalls and achieving a soul-satisfying relationship.

The Oxytocin Connection

Touch creates connection. And recent research has demonstrated that this phenomenon has a chemical basis.

Our bodies produce many neurohormones, chemicals that operate through the nervous system and affect our brains. One that's been getting a lot of press lately is oxytocin. Oxytocin has been touted as the "love hormone," but I'd call it the "feeling bonded hormone." It's released by physical closeness, and makes us feel bonded to the person we're experiencing this closeness with. When a woman gives birth, her body is flooded with oxytocin, making her bond with her newborn. When she nurses, waves of oxytocin strengthen this connection, leaving her utterly in love with her baby. You can see the Divine wisdom here: God wants women to care for their children, and they're more likely to do so if they bond with them.

God also wants husbands and wives to stay together. When a man and woman are physically intimate, therefore, oxytocin is right there, performing its magic, making them feel at one and committed. But intimacy isn't necessary to start the chemical flow; oxytocin is released by any form of physical closeness. Hugging will do it. So will holding hands. In fact, oxytocin is secreted even when two people just *touch*.

Oxytocin would be powerful enough if it only created a sense of bonding. But it does more: It turns off skepticism, caution, and aversion. And it turns on trust. In other words, under the influence of oxytocin, you can kiss your judgment goodbye. Hence a leading neuropsychiatrist's advice to women: "Don't let a guy hug you unless you plan to trust him."*

But why are only women so advised? Because there's a gender difference here: Estrogen, the "female" hormone, increases oxytocin's bonding effect; testosterone, the "male" hormone (also responsible for physical desire), diminishes it. This "oxytocin disparity" is especially pronounced in early adolescence, when estrogen and testosterone levels soar. Consequently, young teenage girls are dangerously vulnerable to the power of touch, and they'll bond, trust, and drop judgment at the drop of a hat. One writer spells it out: "Girls should learn that bonding is a likely effect of physical intimacy — not necessarily a response to the other person. The feeling is, 'He's the only one for me.' But the reality is, 'Because we touched, I now *feel* as if he's the only one for me.' "

Most young teenage boys, on the other hand, while greatly interested in females, have little ability to bond with them — their hormones are leading them more toward conquest than toward connection. What to a girl may feel like love may to a boy be nothing more than another notch on his belt. In other

* This loss of judgment and tendency to trust apparently apply not only to the guy in question. Young women in committed relationships have proven significantly worse than their unattached peers at detecting insincerity in *other* men (Johnson et al., "Female Deception Detection as a Function of Commitment and Self-Awareness").

words, boys and girls "have seriously different priorities" when it comes to relationships. (Along these lines, a renowned psychologist wrote in 1969: "It is a girl's task not to allow herself to be used as a tool. It is a boy's obligation not to use a girl as an object." Old-fashioned — or as valid as ever?)

As males and females mature and their hormones settle down, the gap between their chemical realities narrows somewhat and their needs move closer. Most significantly, men become increasingly interested in and capable of a genuine connection with a woman, especially after marriage. In fact, married men have somewhat less testosterone than bachelors, allowing for a greater oxytocin response, which leads to more bonding and commitment. (It remains unclear whether this is because marriage lowers testosterone levels, or because men with lower testosterone levels are more likely to marry.)

Nevertheless, oxytocin affects females more than males.* If you're female, you can delight in the knowledge that you're chemically more predisposed to feel that wonderful high of connection when your husband touches you.

The problem is when the object of your affections is not — nor is he necessarily planning on becoming — your husband.

---

* Men bond also due to the influence of the hormone vasopressin, which is connected to vigilance and aggression (Kuchinskas, *The Chemistry of Connection*, 17, 121–22). The presence of vasopressin means that, rather than just getting physical, a man generally needs to feel protective of his woman to bond with her. A little danger and excitement also may help (Ibid., 102). (Hence my suggestion for a movie: A young woman, disgruntled with men's casualness about relationships, fakes her own kidnapping and sets up the man of her dreams to rescue her. He bonds with her, and they marry.)

As I said, in addition to bonding, oxytocin shuts down judgment and creates feelings of trust. Physical contact before marriage can therefore be dangerous: It can leave you feeling connected to someone who's all wrong for you or isn't interested in a real relationship. The danger is worse if this person you've bonded with has no scruples. In a book instructing men how to "succeed" with women, the (male) authors essentially counsel their readers to exploit the female oxytocin response to their advantage. On a date, they explain, the woman's sizing up the man, looking for reasons why he's not good enough for her. He therefore has to get physical with her *fast* — because then, instead of looking for reasons why he's *not* the right one, she'll be looking for reasons why he *is*.

For a female, in other words, touch is subliminally manipulative,* and she can end up not just badly hurt but badly used. With enough such experiences, she can lose her personal boundaries and sense of self. One thing's for sure: She won't be happy. Most of those who suffer depression due to romantic involvement are women. When it comes to relationships, women are simply more vulnerable.

Understanding Men

Undoubtedly, testosterone has given guys a pretty bad

---

* In general, women are more easily swayed than men, due to estrogen, and to the fact that more parts of their brains operate simultaneously, resulting in vacillations rather than single-minded thinking (Gurian, *The Wonder of Girls*, 46, 197, 238). These realities, combined with the oxytocin effect, may partially explain the Biblical law absolving a woman of responsibility for being seduced, while punishing the man (Exodus 22:15).

rap. "Boys are animals," one teacher I know tells his female students. "Boys are liars," another warns his. Indeed, men have up to 100 times more testosterone circulating in their bodies than women have, and this hormone switches on a part of the brain twice as large as the corresponding part of a woman's brain. No wonder males are more intent on getting physical with females than vice versa, particularly during adolescence (and some men have quite an extended adolescence). And some definitely will lie ("I really love you," "You can count on me") or at least fudge the truth to get what they want. At the same time, male-bashing is grossly unfair to men, for it reflects only half the story.

The other half is that males, just like females, are *souls* — souls easily distracted by physicality, but souls nonetheless. Chemically, we humans — men and women alike — tie the pleasurable feeling of bonding to the person we experience it with, programming us for monogamy. Ultimately, men want and need the same thing women do: a committed, loving, lifelong relationship with a soul mate. As one writer poetically puts it, "We are both, women and men, from the same lonely planet."

So men have two sides. The question is, which is activated? Here, women — though they may deny it — have more than a little influence. Avi, a sensitive young Israeli man who had recently become religious, described it like this:

> We men have an outer will and an inner will. My outer will is for immediate physical pleasure. When a woman dresses provocatively and isn't *shomer negiah*, I'm drawn after my physical instincts, and we both lose: I don't become who I could be, she doesn't get a guy who's inter-

ested in her for who she is, and neither of us winds up with a spiritually satisfying relationship.

But I also have an inner will. When a woman's dress and behavior compel me to see and relate to her more deeply, she puts me in touch with the part of me that wants and needs the real thing as much as she does. And we both win.

Avi concluded, "Women have more power than they know." Politically correct or not, while men are responsible for themselves, women can help bring out the worst or the best in them.

Women may downplay their role in shaping the male mentality, but men are well aware of it. A friend of mine was on a bus, two rows behind a couple of very immodestly dressed girls. Two boys boarded the bus and took the seats behind them and in front of her. She saw them glance at the girls and then overheard one say quietly to the other, "Look at them — and then they call us animals." Had these girls teasingly informed them that "by the way, we're not *shomer negiah*," the boys would undoubtedly have found it even harder to repress their natural urges.

We females have to face the fact that we often dress and act in a way that encourages men to behave like animals, and then when they do, we condemn them.

But male-bashing is not only unkind to men; it's highly detrimental to women. When we expect guys to be cave men, that's what we get, for they have no higher expectations to meet. So maybe it's time for us to raise the bar, access our higher selves, and credit guys with the ability to access theirs.

Looking Ahead

Someone once asked me, "With all the people you speak to about being *shomer negiah* — high school students and older singles, observant and non-observant — do you ever feel you're wasting your time?"

"Absolutely," I said. "When I speak to people living for the moment."

If you just want to have a good time without giving any thought to tomorrow (to say nothing of a year from now), nothing can possibly inspire you to be *shomer negiah* — or to abstain from drugs, reckless driving, or other risks. While all may ruin your life, they can feel good at the time.

Most intelligent, mature people, however, exercise foresight. They know our experiences make or break us. By the time someone who's been physical with several people finally meets the right one, he or she brings a lot of baggage into that relationship: unwanted memories and comparisons, reduced sensitivity and sense of specialness, and quite possibly an impaired ability to trust. In the words of a famous woman: "Experience is a good teacher, but she sends in terrific bills."

So we have to ask ourselves: Although getting physical may feel good right now, might I regret it?

This is a question for females in particular, as the past affects them more than it does males. The part of the brain responsible for memory, the hippocampus, is larger and more active in women than in men. And the hippocampus also attaches emotions to memories. A woman is thus more likely than a man to remember not just events but how they felt. Thus, a woman's past can be just as real to her as her present.

Unfortunately, looking back at our pasts, many of us — observant or not — don't exactly have fond memories. I was once talking to a secular woman, Jodi, about her young daughter. Knowing what goes on in society, I was worried about this little girl.

"How will you keep your daughter from doing things girls not much older are doing," I asked Jodi, "without some, um — " (here I had to think fast, since she doesn't want to talk about religion) "spiritual structure in your life? Unless, of course," I added, "the idea of her doing that stuff doesn't bother you."

Jodi's eyes widened. "Are you crazy?!" she exclaimed. "The last thing I want my daughter doing is what *I* did as a teenager!" She shuddered. "Ugh, it was so *stupid*."

What was easy and exciting is often what you're most embarrassed by years later. Conversely, things that were hard and less exciting might just be what you're proudest of.

After I spoke at a high school in North America several years ago, a student named Adina came up to me, looking serious. She confessed she'd been debating whether to remain *shomer negiah*, but the idea of not entering marriage with a "past" really spoke to her, and she decided to continue. I was happy for her — although I wondered if she'd be able to stick to her convictions.

A few years later, at the conclusion of a talk I gave in Israel, a glowing young woman came over to me. It was Adina. Her hair was covered by a beautiful scarf.

"I see you got married!" I said with a smile.

"Yes," she said, with an even bigger smile. "And I want to tell you: From the time you spoke to us and I made my decision, I stayed strong and was *shomer negiah* right up until the wedding. I did it!"

"Great!" I congratulated her. "So tell me something, and be honest." I motioned her over to the side and lowered my voice. "All those Saturday nights that your friends were out having 'fun,' and you were, say, going bowling or watching a Disney video with your family — all those 'good times' you missed — was it worth it?"

Adina's eyes lit up. "Oh, *yeah*!"

So many people live for today and make choices they regret. While we can't turn back the clock, we *can* get back a good deal of what we've lost. Women who used to be physically involved with guys, then became religious, report that touching their husbands for the first time was thrilling. But this metamorphosis doesn't occur overnight. It takes time to regain the sensitivity and the sense of specialness your lifelong relationship should have.

Being *shomer negiah* from the start ensures that these precious commodities are never lost.

The Oxytocin *Dis*connection?

A powerful argument against male-female involvement before marriage is the emotional fallout. Both men and women suffer from broken relationships. But what if what "broke" wasn't much of a relationship?

While men don't seem to hurt following a fleeting connection, I've always assumed women do. But for some time, high school and college students have been telling me that a girl can repeatedly "hook up" with guys and forget them as easily as they forget her. "That goes totally against female nature," I've insisted. "A girl who claims she can do that is either in denial or on Prozac." But lately I've been wondering if I'm wrong, and if the explanation for this equal-opportunity desensitization may have a chemical basis — in oxytocin.

Ideally, we learn to produce oxytocin by being cuddled as children, especially in the first three years of life. However, if parents aren't attuned to a baby's needs, or if they're busy most of the day and surrogate parents (such as day care workers) don't provide enough loving physical attention, a child may never develop a strong oxytocin response.* Early emotional deprivation, therefore, may underlie the later phenomenon of getting physical with no emotional bonding.

Fortunately, the brain can grow and change. Through positive adult experiences, even someone neglected in childhood can learn to produce oxytocin. So can *negative* adult experiences cause a *healthy* person to *stop* producing it? A doctor once shared the following with me:

"Did you ever wonder what happens to a woman who's gotten physical with too many men?" he asked. "How can she feel connected not just to one guy she's no longer with, but to another, and another, without suffering an emotional breakdown? She probably can't — so her brain steps in to save her. In each subsequent relationship, the brain secretes less oxytocin. She therefore experiences less bonding in the relationship, and less pain when it ends. In extreme cases, oxytocin activity may cease altogether."

---

* Another contributing factor may be induced labor, which "can overdose the baby with artificial oxytocin, possibly making her brain less sensitive to it" (Kuchinskas, "The Oxytocin Gap"). Similarly, heavy usage of the recreational drug Ecstasy, which artificially releases oxytocin, can impair the body's natural oxytocin response (Kuchinkas, "Recovering from MDMA Burnout").

In other words, if a woman involves herself with too many guys, she can turn into one.

"The problem is," he continued, "when such a woman finally meets the right man, her oxytocin levels are on the floor, so she can't forge the same hormonal bond with him as she once could have. She's killed her own oxytocin response."

This theory of decreasing oxytocin — promoted, I discovered, by people with a strong conservative agenda — had been slammed by several researchers, one of whom called it "complete pseudoscience." Since these researchers may have their own liberal agenda, I asked Susan Kuchinskas, author of *The Chemistry of Connection*, for her opinion. She replied that the theory being popularized states that oxytocin can be "used up" in casual premarital relationships, leaving an inadequate amount for marriage. This, she says, doesn't make sense. Take the mother-child relationship: Mothers don't use up their oxytocin on their first child; they remain capable of bonding with additional children.

But what if that first mother-child relationship terminates painfully? I heard about a Holocaust survivor's daughter, born after the war, whose mother was emotionally detached from her. She later discovered that, while in a concentration camp, her mother had given birth to a baby who was immediately murdered. Apparently this trauma destroyed her ability to bond with her next child. Could painful male-female break-ups similarly impair bonding?

According to Susan Kuchinskas, quite possibly: "Think of the oxytocin response as a habit, a learned response to stimuli. Certainly habits can be broken or changed." In other words, if a woman learns that the "habit" of secreting oxytocin causes her pain, she may adapt by secreting less. Kuchinskas therefore states: "I agree with you that there is a hormonal — or neurochemical — explanation for some women's and men's ability to hook up without feeling bonded." And part of that explanation may be too much hooking up.

The idea that premarital relationships may impair our oxytocin response is only a theory. But if proven true, it will give us a great deal more insight into what God has in mind in asking us to be *shomer negiah*.*

The "Relationships Altogether" Question

When I speak in a high school where dating is the norm, I try to discuss only *negiah*, skirting the larger issue of boy-girl relationships. But when it inevitably comes up, I don't mince words.

At the end of one of my talks, sixteen-year-old Helena asked pointedly, "So when do you think I should start dating?"

"Do you intend to be *shomer negiah*?" I asked her just as pointedly.

"Yes."

"When do you think you'll be ready for marriage?"

"Probably when I'm around twenty-one."

"How long do you think you could go out with a guy you're feeling closer and closer to and still be *shomer negiah*?"

Helena thought a moment. "Maybe six months."

"So start dating when you're twenty and a half."

---

* And if proven true, it's reasonable to believe that just as emotional sensitivity can rebound with time, so can the oxytocin response.

At least Helena thought about timing a relationship before becoming involved in it. Other people don't. Once, after I spoke on a program for semi-observant college students, a young woman introduced herself as Dana.

"My boyfriend and I have decided to try becoming *shomer negiah*," she told me. "We're hoping you can help us get started."

"I'd be happy to, if I can," I replied. "Tell me a little about your relationship."

"Well, we're very close," Dana began. "We're both sophomores at the same university and have the same major, so we attend many of the same classes. We often study together. In fact, we probably spend most of our waking hours together. We plan to get married in two and a half years, after graduation. We really love each other.

She paused. "So what practical advice can you give us about how to be *shomer negiah*?"

I shook my head sympathetically. "Beats me."

Being *shomer negiah* is intended for a relatively brief period prior to marriage. Once you've found the right person, set a date for as soon as possible. Otherwise, you're asking for trouble.

I once got a letter from a very distressed young girl. "I became friendly with a boy when I was twelve," Shira wrote. "We were just friends for nearly two years. But lately we've realized we have stronger feelings for each other. This is not some teenage infatuation — we're more mature than most people our age. We know and genuinely love each other deeply. And we're certain we're right for each other.

"The problem is, we're only fourteen — and I can't imagine getting married until I'm at least twenty. We've been *shomer negiah* and want to continue. But how are we supposed to not touch each other for the next six years?!"

What could I possibly tell Shira? Break up, and pick things up in five and a half years? Don't break up, but hardly see each other, and meet only in broad daylight and in crowded places? Any practical answer would be emotionally unacceptable.

Yet staying in a long-term relationship and hoping to remain *shomer negiah* is equally impractical. Even dating for a shorter period but spending too much time together can send the best of intentions down the drain. This happened to a nearly engaged couple I know — and although they recommitted to being *shomer negiah*, they had to deal with mutual blame, mistrust, and loss of respect in the wake of what had happened. Setbacks like this can derail a relationship.

Then there are negative consequences of a different sort. I know of a *shomer negiah* couple who were seeing far too much of each other during their very long engagement. The tension grew unbearable — so they adopted a desperate coping mechanism: They shut off the romantic energy between them and began relating as brother and sister. After marrying, they had major problems getting the romance back.

Furthermore, whether or not you're *shomer negiah* — and especially if you aren't — long-term premarital relationships can leave you emotionally attached to someone you're not meant to marry. A distraught young woman once called me with this problem: She's nineteen, she said, and has had a boyfriend for three years. Now she's starting to think about marriage — and it's clear that this guy is not the one. At the same time, she loves him and can't imagine leaving him.

She's torn. What should she do?

Obviously, she can't marry the wrong person because of an emotional attachment. There's no choice but to say a sad goodbye to Mr. Wrong and hope to find Mr. Right. But what a shame that she invested so much in a relationship that wasn't meant to be — and how painful to break up.

"But he *could* have been the right guy," a girl may protest. True. And you can jump into a physical relationship with a guy you barely know, and he *could* really be your soul mate. For that matter, you can cross a busy street blindfolded and *could* make it safely to the other side. But we don't live that way.

The kinds of problems I've described are why it's wise to sidestep boy-girl relationships — including social interactions that could lead to them — until you're ready for marriage. And don't think, in all innocence, "What could be wrong with just getting a guy/girl to notice me?" Everything starts somewhere. Getting noticed can lead to being given someone's cell phone number, which can lead to text messaging, which can lead to talking on the phone, which can lead to talking in well-lit, public places, which can lead to talking in *not*-well-lit, *not* public places, which can lead to *not* talking... As a friend of mine says, "Every office affair begins with a casual conversation at the water cooler."

In addition, believe it or not, gazing into someone's eyes, connecting emotionally, or even just friendly interaction causes a feel-good oxytocin response. In other words, females bond just by talking. (Ever wonder why teenage girls spend so much time on the phone?) Plus the guy may interpret it as more than talking: One study found that when a man observes a man and woman conversing, the areas of his brain governing physical desire are activated. What women see as an innocent conversation, men perceive as a potential physical encounter.* The upshot: There's nothing simple about male-female interaction — and, as I've tried to show, about where it leads. Particularly if you intend to be *shomer negiah*, it's smart to socialize only with the same sex until you're ready for the real thing.

What We Really Need

As I said, we often *feel* close when we really crave to *be* close. In other words, preoccupation with physicality frequently masks a deeper, unfulfilled need for genuine connection. A woman named Laura recounted something touching that drove this point home:

"I started becoming observant when I was sixteen. In my coed high school, there was all this pressure to be part of the boy-girl scene, and I couldn't resist it. So I promised myself I would date only Jewish boys — and I would be *shomer negiah*. Of course, when a Jewish boy asked me out, I wouldn't tell him I was *shomer negiah*, because he'd probably never heard of such a thing and wouldn't know what to make of it — or me.

---

* Interestingly, when a man and woman converse, the man's cognitive performance declines — and the more attractive he finds her, the stupider he gets. Researchers suspect that his trying to impress her depletes his mental resources (Karremans, "Interacting with Women Can Impair Men's Cognitive Functioning"; see also Kaufman, "Interacting with Women Makes Men Stupid"). This phenomenon may be a good argument for single-sex education — and for a yeshivah student not to spend time in female company before going back to his studies.

"So at the end of the date, he'd walk me up to my front door and expect a goodnight kiss. But I had it all worked out: I'd smile and say, 'Just a minute,' disappear into the house, and reappear with a bag of chocolate chip cookies I'd baked earlier that day, with a ribbon around it and a note attached. In my cutest voice I'd say, 'Can I give you these instead?'

"And you know what?" Laura continued with a conspiratorial smile. "I always got asked out again."

Either boys really like chocolate chip cookies, or the fact that she was thinking of them earlier in the day, and had taken the time to bake them cookies and write a little note, meant more to them than a kiss.

We think we need physicality. We do — but far more, we need love. That's perhaps the most important thing we can learn from being *shomer negiah*.

Why Not Once We're Engaged?

Suppose you had every intention of playing by the rules until the wedding (as Jewish law dictates), but now you're engaged and feel your resolve weakening. "We've been good," you tell yourself, "and we've reaped the benefits: We've maintained our objectivity and have developed the beginnings of true love. At this point, would it be so terrible if we stopped being *shomer negiah*?"

In Judaism, we use the physical to express the spiritual. When we dress in a way that reflects our souls, our bodies become holy. Likewise, when we engage in a physical relationship to express a spiritual bond, physicality becomes holy.

The question is, what determines this spiritual bond? You might assume it's love. But Judaism says there's something higher.

Two scenarios:

One: You've been going out with someone for a long time. He or she looks into your eyes and says sincerely, "I love you...but I can't commit."

Two: You've been going out with someone for not such a long time. He or she looks into your eyes and says sincerely, "I haven't known you long enough to say 'I love you.' But I want to spend the rest of my life with you."

Which scenario moves you more?

As powerful as love is, if it lacks commitment, it lacks holiness. Commitment, Judaism teaches, is the all-powerful bond that sanctifies physicality. And commitment means not just the intention to marry, but the real thing: marriage itself. Marriage transforms a relationship, including our physical union, into something Godly.

Years ago, when I couldn't imagine marrying someone I didn't at least think I loved, my friend Jamie got engaged to a man she hadn't known for long. I was surprised. "Do you love each other?" I wanted to know.

"Not yet," Jamie replied.

I was taken aback. "But you feel ready to get married?"

"Absolutely. My fiancé is a major mensch. Beyond that, we really like, respect, admire, and appreciate each other. We enjoy being together. We have great communication. We have the same values and life goals. And we're physically attracted. We have all the ingredients necessary for love but one: enough time spent together. We could continue going out until we love each other and then get married; or we can go ahead now, knowing that the love will soon be there. If we know it's right," Jamie concluded, "why wait?"

Unlike an unmarried couple who love each other, from

the moment my friend and her fiancé married, their physical bond was holy. Needless to say, the love came — and today they have a beautiful marriage. Love doesn't always lead to commitment, but commitment leads to love.

A couple may deeply love each other and know they're soul mates, but until they marry, they're spiritually separate. Since the physical is meant to express the spiritual, they must remain physically separate as well. When they finally stand under the *chuppah* (wedding canopy) and enter a spiritual union, their souls finally "touch" — and so can their bodies.*

When I was thirteen, I started hearing more and more about divorce. Concerned, I asked my mother, "Mommy, do you think you and Daddy will ever get divorced?"

My mother and father looked at each other lovingly. "I don't think so," my mother said with a smile.

I was relieved.

Years later, as a mother myself, I was asked essentially the same question. "Imma," my eleven-year-old daughter began out of the blue, "when a mother and father get divorced, who gets the kids?"

I was taken aback. "Well, sweetheart, it depends," I answered cautiously. "But why are you asking?"

My daughter shrugged nonchalantly. "Just because."

"Are you worried that Abba and I will get divorced some day?"

---

* How do you know the two of you will be physically compatible if you haven't tried things out first? This question is addressed in *The Magic Touch*.

"No."

"I'm not either," I said reassuringly.

But my little girl didn't look relieved.

Realizing she needed more explanation than I myself once had, I asked, "Do you want to know why?"

"Yes," she replied, a bit too eagerly.

I thought a moment. "When people divorce, they usually say, 'We don't love each other anymore.' But because of how Abba and I dated, the part of each other we saw and started to love was who we each really were. And you know what? As we get older, lots of things change, but who we are usually doesn't. That means we'll probably always love each other. So I don't think we'll get divorced."

In other words: Love won't disappear if it's based on something permanent. That answer satisfied my daughter — and hopefully it was educational as well. For now that she's older and has learned about being *shomer negiah*, maybe she'll recall this conversation, understand "how Abba and I dated," and know that in this crazy world, there's a way of relating that allows true love to develop and last.

Appreciating someone for his or her inner self is a skill — and the best way to acquire it is by learning to appreciate yourself for who you are. Having talked about loving another, then, let's turn to the even more complex topic of loving yourself — which is based on a quality called *tzniut*.

PART TWO
LOVING YOURSELF

One of the most powerful ideas and practices in Jewish life is something called *tzniut*. While commonly translated as modesty, *tzniut* is more accurately understood as internal self-definition. Its purpose is to help us recognize and appreciate our inner goodness — our souls. *Tzniut* is therefore the basis of healthy self-love.

Tzniut is incumbent upon both sexes. Whenever we let the outside overshadow the inside — whether by dressing provocatively or by ostentatiously zooming around in a flashy sports car — we sink into superficiality and disconnect from our deeper selves. When we instead focus on the internal, we build ourselves spiritually.

While crucial for men, *tzniut* is emphasized for women. Because the female body is more obviously sensual, women are at greater risk of devaluing themselves by dressing to attract men and ultimately equating self-worth with appearance. At the same time, Jewish tradition (Genesis *Rabbah* 2:18) teaches that God created women with a greater propensity for *tzniut*, should they choose to plug into it. Judaism views the physical as reflecting the spiritual. The defining feature of the female body is internal, pointing to the more internal nature of the female soul. Hence women's generally greater sensitivity to privacy and embarrassment at inappropriate self-revelation. Just as parents will be more intent on providing art lessons for an artistic child, women should be encouraged to develop their gift of *tzniut*.

Much of the following chapters, therefore, focuses on women. Yet men should keep reading, so they can better understand the tremendous benefits of women's — including their wives' — fully internalizing *tzniut*.

Chapter 3, "The Core Connection," develops the ideas in my book *Outside/Inside: A Fresh Look at Tzniut** and offers additional perspectives on this fundamental concept. Chapter 4, "Saying No to the Media," discusses the media's damage to self-image and the necessity of minimizing media influence in order to live spiritually wholesome lives. Chapter 5, "Ending the Hunger for Selfhood," describes how *tzniut* is crucial in preventing and curing eating disorders and in creating positive feelings toward our bodies and ourselves. Together, these chapters will help you find, appreciate, and — most important — love yourself.

---

* *Outside/Inside* offers a spiritual understanding of *tzniut* and its impact on our lives. I highly recommend reading it before reading the following chapters. In any case, I open Chapter 3 with a brief review of the book's central theme.

3
The Core Connection

When author Wendy Shalit first heard someone say "*Tzniut*," she responded, "God bless you," thinking he had sneezed! Given that others respond to the term with, "Ugh, you mean that oppressive dress code for Orthodox women?" I found Shalit's innocent reaction refreshing. Even more refreshing, however, would be to hear, "You mean that great Jewish idea that liberates us from superficiality and gives us our personhood?"

What Is *Tzniut*?*

Contrary to popular belief, *tzniut* is not just about what we wear, but about who we are. It begins with the simple

* For a fuller discussion of these and many other ideas — including women's greater connection to *tzniut*, *tzniut*'s transformative power, how *tzniut* fuels love, and the importance of individuality — see *Outside/Inside.*

awareness that the physical world can be misleading, and that to find truth, we must look deeper, past our own bodies. It means realizing that we are more than skin-deep and that we want to see ourselves, and be seen, for who we are — not for our looks or even for our talents, abilities, and accomplishments, which are mere external expressions of our essence. The real person is the goodness within. In Jewish terms: We are souls, made in God's image.

Tzniut conveys this soul-consciousness to the world. One primary way of sending the message is through dress.

Adam and Eve needed no clothing, the Torah tells us (Genesis 2:25), because they were incapable of viewing each other only physically. Their bodies paled amid the radiance of their souls. After their terrible mistake in the Garden of Eden, however, the soul's light dimmed, and in the ensuing darkness, imagination took over. Suddenly it appeared as if the body were the real self. Adam and Eve's instinctive reaction was to clothe themselves. Why? What exactly is the purpose of clothing?

Think of how you would care for a precious pearl. You wouldn't leave it sitting out on a shelf — you'd put it in a box. This box would have a simple, quality look. It would be attractive, maybe even beautiful. But you wouldn't want it to outshine the pearl. A box's understated beauty reminds us that its value comes not from itself, but from its contents. This kind of beauty beckons us to look inside.

So too with body and soul. *Tzniut* means recognizing that although my body is a beautiful gift from God, it's merely a container, so it mustn't distract from what it contains. When I clothe my body attractively but not eye-catchingly, I draw attention to who I am inside, where my self-worth lies. Clothing prevents my body from overpowering my true identity.

Tzniut, therefore, is the art of downplaying our bodies in favor of our essence. It reminds us all that we are more than meets the eye.

Yet *tzniut* doesn't mean looking drab. A pearl doesn't belong in a shabby, cardboard box. Rather, just as the pearl box reflects the preciousness of the pearl, the body clothed with *tzniut* should reflect the beauty of the soul.

We see this idea in how the Torah describes Adam and Eve's clothing. God made them "garments of leather" (Genesis 3:21). *Ohr*, leather, begins with the letter *ayin*, phonetically interchangeable with *alef*. When *ohr* is spelled with an *alef*, the phrase reads "garments of light." Clothing enables us to shine God's light into a darkened world.

It is therefore important that we choose our clothing carefully. The Hebrew word for "garment" is *beged*, from the same root as *boged*, "betray." Clothing can cover us, as a garment is meant to do, or it can overemphasize our bodies, thus betraying our deeper selves.

For those of us who have grown up in secular society, it can initially be daunting not to accentuate our physical selves. We may suddenly feel invisible. And we may worry: What if my inner beauty doesn't shine through? What if I don't have any?

The good news is that *everyone* has his or her unique inner beauty — and the more we focus on and nurture it, the more it blossoms, affecting everyone around us.

Refraining from physical self-display also promotes personal freedom. No longer slaves to fashion, we can be true to ourselves. *Tzniut*, in the words of one teenager, can give you the clarity, self-confidence, and courage to "veer off the track of conformity and head into a life you know is right."

Tzniut transcends dress. It includes how we present ourselves, speak, behave, and interact. In every aspect of life, *tzniut* means shunning superficiality in favor of depth and spirituality. *Tzniut* isn't just a way of dressing. It's a way of being.

The Looking-Glass Self

Tzniut means encouraging others to see me as I am. But if I know who I am, who cares how others see me?

No matter how much we think we know who we are, our sense of self is greatly impacted by our interactions. The resulting self-image could be called the "looking-glass self," formed by others' impressions of us. In short: "I am who I think you think I am" — how others see me is how I come to see myself. If so, it's crucial that our interactions strengthen who we really are.

The problem is when they don't. A woman whose provocative dress draws appreciative gazes and comments from men will dress even more provocatively. Even if she doesn't find this attention flattering, the more of it her image elicits, the more she'll define herself physically, and the more her spiritual self will suffer.

Alternatively, when a woman's attire commands respect, she'll dress even more respectably — and her spiritual self-image will strengthen.

I first came to Israel in jeans and a backpack, looking like the free-spirited American tourist I was. I remember walking through the market in Jerusalem's Old City and being hassled by young shopkeepers in broken English: "Hey, come here! You so cute, I give you half price. You come for coffee?" I wasn't the least bit flattered. Still, being treated like an object, it was hard not to feel like one.

I soon encountered Judaism and started becoming observant. One warm, spring day, while my friend Tova and I were hiking alone in the barren West Bank hills outside Jerusalem, some local men suddenly materialized out of nowhere. Obviously, this story could have ended badly. Fortunately, however, these guys responded to social cues such as dress. They must have thought: *If these strange girls are wearing skirts, sleeves, and socks on such a warm day, they must be religious, and there's no point in starting up with them.* One of them then told us with concern, "You know, you shouldn't walk around here by yourselves," and they insisted on accompanying us back toward the city.

I'm not convinced these men would have treated us so respectfully had we been dressed less religiously.*

My point here isn't just that how we dressed affected how we were treated. When these men spoke to us so nicely, I felt like a person instead of a potential pick-up. My self-image subtly shifted another step away from how I'd felt as a secular tourist. And my commitment to *tzniut* increased.

Kicking the Attention Habit

So what stands between us and *tzniut*? As much as we may want the deeper self-image *tzniut* gives us, many of us fear that if we stop flaunting ourselves, we'll no longer get attention — and that can be painful, especially for young

* This is not to absolve men of responsibility for their behavior, no matter how women dress.

singles. The question is: What kind of attention?

I once saw a comedy skit in which three attractive, provocatively dressed women enter a restaurant, while a barbaric-looking man stands outside. He leers and motions crudely to two of the women, dismissing the third, to her dismay. The ladies sit down at a table, and he continues leering and motioning through the window, still ignoring the third. This poor woman gets more and more upset. She doesn't want to date this Neanderthal or even talk to him, but he sure had better think she looks good!

It's amazing how many females believe it's "better to be looked over than overlooked," making their self-esteem dependent on the attention of random males. What's worse, after "playing" with attention-seeking girls, these guys often laugh at them behind their backs. This phenomenon is by no means new. Listen to nineteen-year-old Laurie (a boy) talking to Jo (a girl) in the classic *Little Women*, published in 1868:

> I'm glad you can't flirt; it's really refreshing to see a sensible, straightforward girl who can be jolly and kind without making a fool of herself. Between ourselves, Jo, some of the girls I know really do go on at such a rate I'm ashamed of them. They don't mean any harm, I'm sure; but if they knew how we fellows talk about them afterward, they'd mend their ways, I fancy.... We don't like romps and flirts, though we may act as if we did sometimes. The pretty, modest girls are never talked about, except respectfully, among gentlemen. Bless your innocent soul, if you could be in my place for a month you'd see things that would astonish you a trifle.

If anyone were "astonished" by anything anymore, girls today would surely be more than "a trifle" astonished at what boys say about them. Yet many women still need to be noticed, no matter by whom.

Several years ago, the BBC presented a radio program on "fundamentalist religions," and somehow I was chosen to represent "fundamentalist" (i.e., Orthodox) Jewish women.

"Why," the interviewer asked me, "do you Orthodox Jewish women cover up so much?"

Inwardly, I prayed, "God, please give me a good one-liner." Then I looked straight at him and said, "Because I don't want to be invisible."

He looked puzzled. I knew he was thinking: *But that's backward. Covering up makes a woman invisible.*

"If I were to wear less," I continued, "my physical self would be obvious, but my inner self would be lost. When I dress like this, I'm visible."

We all want to be visible. To this man, "visible" meant being noticed. To me, "visible" means being *seen*. Being noticed has to do with what you have; being seen relates to who you are. Like men, women too have an "outer will" and an "inner will": Our outer will is to be noticed; our inner will is to be seen.

My friend Karen was working in a restaurant when she became interested in Judaism. *Tzniut* really spoke to her, so she started appearing at work in skirts, longer sleeves, etc. Her male coworkers didn't know what to make of her — no other woman they knew dressed that way. They began paying less attention to her. Or so she thought.

Eventually Karen left her job. A few weeks later, one of the waitresses called her. "You saw how all the guys we worked with were always flirting with us but not with you? Well, after you quit, no fewer than *seven* of them told me, '*She*'s the kind of girl I want to *marry*.'"

Guys believe in different girls for different life stages: The ones who flaunt themselves physically are for fliritng with, while the "quality" girls are marriage material. Of course, guys are mistaken. *Every girl is a quality girl.* Some just don't know it or show it. Girls with *tzniut* may get less attention, but they're more likely to be seen, which is the first step to being loved.

Mixed Messages

Women don't really want to be objectified, yet, as I've said, some find it difficult to forego the attention. So they resort to mixed messages.

For example, many powerful and accomplished women still dress provocatively. This mixed message says: "Be distracted by my looks, but see my brains." Any guy will tell you that's virtually impossible.

When I was an undergraduate at Yale, photographers from a certain disreputable magazine came to campus to shoot "Women of the Ivy League." They set up a studio and advertised for applicants. I was sure they were wasting their time at my university, where women prided themselves on their intellects. But I was wrong. Despite feminist protest, women eagerly posed.

Why? My guess is that most wanted to proudly proclaim: "Yes, I'm an Ivy League woman, and I'm brainy — *but that's not all!*"

But was this request to "appreciate my body *and* my brains" heard? I somehow suspect that the men who checked out "Women of the Ivy League" had little interest in brains. I don't think a bunch of fraternity guys were flipping through the magazine, excitedly commenting, "Hey, look at this one — you think she'll be going for a Ph.D.?" or "Boy, I'd sure like to discuss philosophy with *her*!" These women's intelligence was just a gimmick. Whenever bodies are on display, they eclipse brains.

Then there are provocative dressers who enjoy attracting attention and then chide men for giving it to them. Some even wear T-shirts admonishing guys to stop staring. This mixed message says: "Look, but don't look!" Besides being demeaning and unfair to men, this behavior is an exercise in self-objectification.

I once saw a woman wearing a T-shirt featuring an arrow pointing upward and the words "My face is up there!" I said to her, "You know, there's another way you can get guys to look at your face."

"How?" she asked.

"By wearing a looser shirt."

She smiled broadly. "But that wouldn't be as much fun."

Apparently the main thing is to have fun — whatever the cost.

Then there are ostensibly observant women who dress the part but radiate something different. This mixed message says: "I'm religious — but don't let that stop you from trying." Women like this are often looking for affirmation and approval in the wrong places.

Chava, who attends one of the most right-wing religious high schools in Jerusalem, confided to me that she had caught the eye of a local bus driver (who happened to be married), who was aggressively flirting with her. I was shocked — and stupefied. Of all the women who ride buses in this city, why would this driver start up with a girl wearing a tight ponytail, a buttoned-up blouse, and a mid-calf skirt?

"I give off a certain sensual energy," Chava confessed. "I can't help it."

Okay, so she was "helpless." But once she saw she was getting inappropriate attention, was she helpless to discourage it?

Chava was a "good religious girl" on the outside — but less so on the inside. And her body language gave her away. A dress code doesn't guarantee *tzniut,* the sense of self that frees you from needing cheap external validation. In the words of another high school girl, "You can't just do *tzniut.* You have to also **be** *tzniut.*"

All these mixed messages betray confusion about who we are and how we want to be seen. But with consciousness and effort, we can get past it. One woman I know would mentally tell every man who passed her, "I don't need you to look at me to feel good about myself" — and it worked. Eventually, she both internalized and broadcasted one clear message: *Size me up by the size of my heart.*

The Private World

Some people reject *tzniut* because they misunderstand it. "Earlier generations had hang-ups about their bodies," a pregnant young woman in a skin-tight shirt told a rabbi. "We don't." She's missed the point. *Tzniut* doesn't mean being ashamed of your body; it means being ashamed of being seen as nothing more. In the words of one girl, "It's that small voice that tells you, *this isn't me!*"

Tzniut means the body is something special, not to be

shared with just anyone. It means having a sense of privacy.

This sense, sadly, is fading fast. While we're not wearing less than we did a generation ago, we're wearing it with far less privacy. I attended a coed, public high school with no dress code. A girl or guy could come to class wearing as little as they liked. But if any of their undergarments showed, they would have been mortified and would have quickly tucked them in or covered them up. Today, females and males alike let it all hang out.

Showing off one's underwear erases the distinction between public and private. So does the overuse of cell phones, thanks to which there's no longer such thing as a private conversation. One author notes that as a child, "I used to sit on the bus, look at the other passengers, and imagine, 'Who are they? What's happening in their lives?' But now," he writes wistfully, "there's little left to imagine. I just listen to them talking on their cell phones."

Cell phone users often don't realize how embarrassing their conversations are. Sometimes I've wanted to say, "Excuse me — can you maybe keep your personal life personal?" Such as when a young woman walks down the street shouting into her phone, "I was never so humiliated in my life! How could she have told the whole class about my nose job? ...You can't hear me? I SAID, HOW COULD SHE HAVE TOLD THE WHOLE CLASS…?"

Whereas cell phones have eroded privacy, television has destroyed it. Popular news shows, talk shows, and reality shows all expose and sensationalize people's private lives. Exhibitionism has become big entertainment.

The result is desensitization — and confusion about relationships. When we don't know whether an article of clothing, a conversation, or an experience is public or private, it's harder to know the same about a part of our body, a feeling, or a touch. In the words of one expert, "When underwear becomes outerwear...adolescents of both sexes are likely to become confused about the nature of intimacy." *Tzniut* restores the line between public and private, making intimate relationships — including with ourselves — possible.

The Irreplaceable Mom

As her daughter's primary female role model, a mother is all-important in helping her daughter understand herself as a woman. This responsibility is awesome, especially given the media onslaught competing for our daughters' self-image (see the next chapter).

While chatting with Julie, an American woman I know from years back, I asked about her children and their extracurricular activities. She told me her six-year-old daughter was a cheerleader. *Already?* I was taken aback.

"Who is she cheering for?" I asked in wonder.

"The first-grade football players," Julie calmly replied.

I couldn't believe it. "I know you're not religious," I said cautiously, "but don't you have enough feminist in you to object to your daughter being socialized into the role of cheering on the boys in a short skirt at age six?"

"I wasn't happy about it," Julie admitted. "But I did put my foot down when she came home with a cheer that showed the crowd how to 'shake your thing.' I went to the coach and told her, 'I'm sorry, but I don't want my little daughter to know she *has* a 'thing,' and I *certainly* don't want her shaking it.' So the coach removed that cheer from the list."

Good for you, I silently applauded.

"And you know what?" she continued. "Within a few days, five other mothers called me and said, 'Thanks for speaking up. We wanted to, but we were afraid of sounding like prudes.'"

Oy.

Amid increasing objectification of females, mothers — and fathers — may be their daughters' only defense. If we abandon them for fear of "prudishness," they're lost. So let's be clear: We're not being uptight; we're protecting our daughters' personhood. And that may mean not letting them do something spiritually unhealthy. But our best bet is to imbue them right from the start with *tzniut* — internal self-definition, strong belief in themselves, and conviction about their true worth — while modeling it ourselves. Then we just may save them.

In encouraging our young daughters' sense of self, we also allow them a childhood. As we've seen, *tzniut* promotes privacy, and more things should be kept private from children than from adults. This belief traditionally prevented parents from exposing their children to certain things, thereby distinguishing the child's world from the adult world and safeguarding their childhood. Today, however, childhood is disappearing. Children are becoming mini-adults, knowing too much too soon and not knowing how to handle it. In valuing privacy, we reclaim their childhood, shielding them from unnecessary and even harmful exposure and creating a sheltered space in which they can discover and build themselves in healthy ways.

Girls in particular benefit from this protection. Females usually have a greater sense of privacy than males, and experience greater discomfort or even embarrassment when this privacy is violated (leading one modesty advocate to declare: "A society that has declared war on embarrassment is one that is hostile to women"). Furthermore, beginning in adolescence, females fall prey to what feminists call the "male gaze." The minute a girl becomes aware of how males can and do view her, she becomes self-conscious and loses her freedom just to be. Suddenly she has to impress — or avoid — boys. As one seventeen-year-old girl put it: "For most teenage girls, guys are everything. Boys validate their existence."*

Girls acquire boy-consciousness soon enough; if anything, we should delay it. I read a disturbing description of an eight-year-old girl imitating a prom queen by dancing and shouting, "Hey, boys, look at me! Look at me, boys! ...[Aren't I] so cute?" At age eight, a girl shouldn't be think-

---

* This syndrome may be one of the strongest arguments for single-sex education. As one researcher views it, girls in all-girl schools lack "that sense of physical vulnerability — of knowing that your [male] peers are publicly sizing you up and finding you either desirable or defective." Instead, these girls "validate their own existence and define their own standing in the world" (Levine, *Mystics, Mavericks, and Merrymakers*, 214). They're more assertive in class, less inhibited, and more confident. Most important, they have a stronger identity (Ibid., 210-1). And those who continue on to women's colleges are more likely to prize their intellects, become leaders, graduate, and pursue advanced degrees (Steinem, *Revolution from Within*, 123, citing A. W. Austin, *Four Critical Years* [San Franciso: Jossey-Bass Higher Education, 1977], 232–3). Women in all-female settings will also ask questions and discuss issues they're uncomfortable bringing up in front of men, as I have seen time after time in addressing all-female versus mixed audiences.

ing about whether boys are noticing her, or what *they're* thinking. She should still be a child.

Where *tzniut* thrives, so does childhood. The premature boy-awareness and self-consciousness of young girls today is strikingly absent in communities where *tzniut* is valued — and particularly where education is single-sex. Instead of prematurely becoming women, girls remain girls longer. A young woman who spent time with the Lubavitch community of Crown Heights writes: "For months, I have been pacing my apartment, trying to corner the most essential reason for the Lubavitch teens' surprising disinhibition. Then it dawned on me: they're like elementary school girls, who run and scream and say it like it is, with no fear that their behavior will hurt them in the realm of [male-female relationships]." Boys' opinions simply don't figure in their self-esteem.

"Children are the living messages we send to a time we will not see," writes one authority on childhood. Our children can be messages of weakness or strength. When parents protect their daughters from objectification and allow them to remain children, they're less likely to discover how to please boys before discovering themselves. In promoting *tzniut*, we allow a girl to keep "saying it like it is" and be who she is.

Tzniut versus Style

Encouraging a girl to be true to herself means helping her consider different ways of doing so. I was speaking at a religious girls' high school when one student raised her hand. "Our school expects us to dress in a certain style," she said. "But is that the only way to express *tzniut*?"

Tzniut doesn't mean uniformity. While it means dressing as a person (as opposed to a body),* you're free to choose what *kind* of person. Still, many schools enforce a particular "look," deeming it the only form of *tzniut*. I appreciated this school's look and didn't want to undermine it. Yet an honest question deserved an honest answer. I took a deep breath.

"The truth is, there are many ways to dress with *tzniut*," I told her. "Take someone I know: Like other women in her community, she wears a loose, long shirt over a flowing skirt with wide pants underneath and a colorful kerchief hanging down her back. Is that *tzniut*? Absolutely! She's appropriately covered and not showing off her body. But the earthy-religious look is very different from the one your school wants.

"Your principal has chosen a school dress code designed to inculcate a certain self-image — and it's unquestionably a lovely and highly self-respecting one. As long as you're here, you have to honor that, just as an employee has to honor the dress code of his or her workplace. But when you graduate, you can decide upon your own style of *tzniut*."

Equating *tzniut* with a particular style not only squelches individuality, but may lead a girl who rejects the style to reject *tzniut* as well. On the other hand, allowing for different tastes frees a girl to express herself as the kind of person she is and wants to be.

It's equally important to differentiate between *tzniut* and style in personality. *Tzniut* needn't mean being quiet and demure, as some may think; there's room for extroverts as

---

* This means, minimally, that your clothing covers your torso, upper arms, and upper legs, including knees; and that it's not sheer, tight, or flashy (according to your community's norms).

well. You just have to make sure you're not seeking the limelight (which is as antithetical to *tzniut* as attention-getting dress) and act appropriately.

I gave up limelight-seeking fairly early, but learning to be appropriate was tougher. I once briefly dated someone who brought me to the home of his very traditional rabbi for Shabbat lunch. At one point the rabbi spilled a cup of grape juice. "And we thought the plastic tablecloth was for the kids!" I joked. He smiled, but I could tell I'd said the wrong thing.

Tzniut, as I later learned, includes discretion. You don't have to change; you just have to tune in to what's appropriate when. Even the most enthusiastic dancer won't perform in the middle of a math class — but she shouldn't stop dancing. While *tzniut* means aspiring to a more spiritual, higher self (and therefore excludes coarse or unrefined behavior), that self must be my own.

The Challenge for Men

Newcomers to Judaism often believe *tzniut* makes demands only of women. Yet its demands on men are just as great if not greater. While a woman must be careful about the kind of attention she elicits from men, a man must be careful about how he looks at women — and that's a tall order.

This obligation is called *shmirat einayim*, "guarding one's eyes." A man isn't permitted to gaze at a revealingly or provocatively dressed woman, or even at a modestly dressed woman if it leads to unkosher thoughts. Many men consequently avoid situations in which they'll likely face this challenge. For example, my husband skirts (no pun intended) the downtown area in the summer, because there's practically nowhere he can safely look. While I can cross a public beach as long as I'm appropriately covered, my husband can't unless he's blind.

Shmirat einayim has at least two reasons, which have actually united two very different constituencies. Some years ago, Jerusalem bus stops were adorned by large advertisements, often featuring immodestly dressed women. Some religious men spray-painted over them, believing that exposure to such pictures undermined their spirituality. Feminists did the same to similar bus stops in the U.S., because they considered such images insulting to women. While their actions may have been questionable, both groups were on target in their sensitivities. Both protecting oneself and respecting females are essential to spirituality — and are reasons for a man to guard his eyes. When a man gazes at a woman inappropriately, he degrades both of them.

In short, while women are responsible for not constituting a "stumbling block" to men, men remain responsible for striving not to stumble — and for seeing women as people, not objects.

Not only is *shmirat einayim* crucial to men's spirituality, but it's also something women really appreciate. I was told of a couple who consulted a marriage counselor. The counselor first asked each of the two what he or she appreciated most about the other. The husband admitted that his wife was very warm and caring. Then it was the wife's turn. "My husband is very near-sighted," she said, "and when we're downtown together in the summer, he takes off his glasses." When the man she's with wants to see only her, a woman feels wonderful.

A man must also think, speak, and act as respectfully as

he "looks." The result can be awe-inspiring. I often speak to secular college students on coed programs that employ religious counselors. Many female participants develop huge crushes on the male counselors, because these young men treat them with such respect. (Sincerely religious men are probably one of Judaism's best advertisements.)

Treating females right isn't difficult if a male simply reminds himself that the object of his interest isn't an object. Imagine you're not the most female-respecting guy, hanging out with a bunch of similar friends, when one spots an attractive girl. With your glasses off, you can't see her clearly, but the others can, and soon they're all rating her looks, making crude remarks, and catcalling to her. Increasingly curious to see this girl for yourself, you put your glasses on.

She's your sister.

The Jewish people is one family. Every Jewish girl is your sister. And every non-Jewish girl is no less a person. Even the most hormone-crazed teenage boy can show some respect.

Bottom line: Although the male brain is wired for visual attraction, a spiritually developed man will strive to relate to a woman's inner self. If he succeeds, he'll be far more capable of a soul-satisfying relationship. (More on this in Final Words: For All Males.)

The Male Self-Image

Men struggle with *tzniut* not only regarding women but in terms of their own self-images. While most men aren't tempted to wear low necklines or short skirts, *tzniut*, as I've said, is not only about dress. It's about not defining oneself externally — and plenty of external definitions have nothing to do with attire.

One of men's greatest temptations is to equate self-worth with a good job and a high standard of living. Just as a woman's self-esteem often comes from her body and the attention it attracts, a man's often rides on money and the power it wields. And sadly, just as a physically self-defined woman can spiritually self-destruct, so can a financially-defined man. He may keep his head on straight while he's still young, but then a mid-life crisis hits. Suddenly he's unfulfilled. Something's missing. Unfortunately, he may mistake that "something" for yet more material comfort, leading to an insatiable desire to possess and consume. He may buy a luxury car, wear only the most expensive suits, patronize only the priciest restaurants, and take extravagant vacations. Or he may embark upon a series of meaningless affairs.

This conquest of women in particular signifies inner emptiness. As one observer comments, " 'Are there any hot girls there?' is shorthand for 'I need to fill an existential hole at the center of my soul' " — and obviously, girls aren't the way to fill it.

Of course, aside from wealth and women, a high-paying job brings status. A prestigious profession proclaims: "I've arrived — you can see by my title and the letters following my name. I am a Man."

But is he?

Someone once asked my friend Ariella if she was ashamed of her husband.

Ariella was puzzled. "What for?"

"For not being a professional — you know, like a doctor or lawyer."

Ariella smiled. "My husband," she said gently, "works

tirelessly for an organization that has changed the lives of thousands of people. He has studied the entire Talmud three times. Although we're far from rich, he gives generously to charity. He's always there for me and our children. And he's one of the most moral, goodhearted, God-centered people I know. Does that answer your question?"

Lending Guys a Hand

Ultimately, a man's spiritual growth is his responsibility. But women can lend a hand. Judaism teaches that we're all responsible for helping one another. If your friend is trying to quit smoking, it's selfish to smoke in front of her. And if a guy is trying not to think about girls, it's selfish to flaunt your body in front of him. Restraining yourself isn't submission to some oppressive regime — it's just being kind.

The Jewish people isn't an aggregate of individuals; it's one big organism, much like the body. If the kidneys malfunction, the whole body suffers. Similarly, when Jewish men malfunction spiritually, the whole Jewish world suffers — especially Jewish women. We all benefit from others being at their best, so why not help each other get there?

This doesn't mean a woman must forfeit being beautiful. Melissa was a very attractive woman new to Judaism and living with a religious family headed by a rabbi. Knowing male guests were expected for Shabbat, she was determined to dress in a non-distracting manner. After a frustrating hour trying on different clothes, she finally emerged from her room wearing a frumpy outfit. The rabbi's wife burst out laughing.

"Where's my gorgeous friend Melissa?" she exclaimed.

"You look ridiculous, and not at all like yourself. Go find something appropriate that makes you feel beautiful."

Provocative, no. Beautiful, yes. Beauty is a gift from God. The question isn't *whether* to look good, but *how*. Real beauty invites the beholder to look at the whole person, inside and out.

"Social *Tzniut*"

As we've seen, *tzniut* is about not just clothing, but consciousness. It's a sensitivity to exposing ourselves — not just physically but emotionally.

"Wait!" you say. "Haven't you been explaining that *tzniut* means concealing the external in order to *reveal* the internal?" Yes — but not indiscriminately. Not "Hey, everyone — come watch me bare my soul!" *Tzniut* is about being seen as a soul, not about your entire soul's being seen. Like our bodies, only limited parts of our inner selves are meant to be shared with the general public. Why?

Bonding is one of our deepest needs. It draws us to family, community, friendships, and eventually our soul mates. Yet we have to be selective. Appropriate, carefully chosen bonds can enrich us immeasurably; indiscriminate ones can wreak havoc, blurring the line between ourselves and others — a line essential to self-knowledge and self-respect, and thus to spiritual well-being.

The antidote to unhealthy bonding is *boundaries*. Boundaries have been dropping out of Western culture — particularly among Americans — since the '60s. We're supposed to be "out there," ready to share anything with anyone. But openness and friendliness can go too far. We need to draw a line.

A boundary serves three purposes: It keeps out what belongs out; it keeps in what belongs in; and in defining which is which, it defines who we are. In creating an inviolate personal space, a boundary protects and fosters our sense of self.

Clothing is a visual boundary. It says: "You can see this much of my outer self and no more. The rest is private. My body is my own."

Behavior too requires boundaries: "You can see this much of my inner self and no more. The rest is private. My thoughts and feelings are my own."

What we're talking about here is *reserve*. I'll be honest: Reserve isn't my favorite word. It sounds so stuffy and stiff. But reserve simply means knowing what to reveal or conceal, when and with whom. It means, when necessary, drawing the line. And especially with the opposite sex, that line has to be clear.

Physical and emotional chemistry between men and women is a constant, even in supposedly platonic relationships. God created us that way. Even when you're sure that you and someone of the opposite sex will forever be just friends (and you're just as sure he or she feels exactly the same), attraction can always develop. As the Talmud succinctly states: "*Ein apotropos le'arayot* — There is no guarantor against illicit relationships" (*Ketubot* 13b). Or, translated more loosely: "You can't be too careful." Indiscriminate bonding can ignite sparks. It's playing with fire.

How do we protect ourselves? By being careful about location, speech, dress, demeanor, body language, eye contact, etc. And this applies as much to men as to women.

Picture this: Sarah Rosenbaum has made an appointment

to discuss a personal issue with someone. She arrives at his house and rings the bell. A man wearing a T-shirt, jeans, and sandals opens the door.

"Hello," she says. "I'm here to meet with Michael Gold."

"Call me Mike!" he says amiably. "You must be Sarah. Come on in!"

With a grand sweeping gesture, he ushers her in, closes the door behind her, and leads her downstairs to the family room. Pointing to the couch, he says, "Curl up with the afghan, and feel at home." Then he settles into a bean-bag chair close by. He removes his glasses and gazes warmly into Sarah's eyes. "So, Sarah, what's on your mind?"

You may find nothing wrong with this scene — Mike's just a casual, friendly guy. I like people like Mike. But if I wanted to discuss something personal with him while keeping my distance, I might have trouble. Everything about him calls out, "No boundaries here!"

Now let's replay the scene, turning Mike into a trained counselor with a measure of professional reserve.

Sarah rings the bell. A woman answers the door.

"Hello," Sarah says. "I'm here to meet with Michael Gold."

"That's my husband," the woman replies pleasantly. "Mike! Your client is here!"

A man comes to the door wearing a button-down shirt, pressed pants, socks, and shoes.

"You must be Sarah Rosenbaum," he says with a smile. "I'm Mr. Gold. Please come in."

While his wife retreats into the study,* Mr. Gold leads

---

* The wife's presence in the home prevents *yichud*, seclusion between a

Sarah into the living room. "Please have a seat," he says. He then seats himself in a chair a few feet away. "So tell me, how can I help you?"

In the replay, Michael Gold is no less welcoming and ready to help. But there's a subtle boundary. Despite discussing something personal, he and Shelley aren't going to *get* personal.

Though they may seem restrictive, behavioral boundaries are actually liberating — just like boundaries in dress. Rather than inhibiting interaction, such boundaries make productive exchange possible, comfortable, and rewarding, because there's no undercurrent of physical provocation. Inappropriate interest is unlikely to develop, since neither party's conduct or dress invites it. With proper boundaries, you can discuss the most intimate issues with a therapist without fear of undesired bonding, because the therapist's behavior says he or she is there in a professional capacity.

Setting boundaries can be difficult. My friend Rachel is very social, and always makes her Shabbat guests — particularly newcomers to Judaism — feel at home. Once, when she was expecting, she and her husband hosted a young man from California. It was his first Shabbat experience, and she went all out to make sure it was positive, including being superfriendly. Her guest had a great time. On his way out, he turned toward Rachel, put his hand on her stomach, smiled warmly, and said, "I think pregnant women are so beautiful." She froze — and suddenly it hit her: "I think I was too friendly."

---

man and woman who aren't immediate family. Unlike other aspects of "social *tzniut*," avoiding *yichud* is mandated by Jewish law.

Had Rachel created boundaries, this young man would never have displayed such (inappropriate) affection. Yet he would have enjoyed his visit just as much.

One rabbi I know is an expert at gracefully setting this kind of boundary. His European origins seem to help him maintain a certain formality and dignity (absent in most Americans) while exhibiting genuine caring. Boundaries with warmth — that's social *tzniut* at its best.

Shining Stars

To achieve greatness — as a boss, a parent, a spouse, or just a human being — it helps immeasurably to have role models. We may not be able to reach the stars, but we can use them as guides. One of my shining "stars" in *tzniut* is Rebbetzin Chaya Sara Kramer (of blessed memory). She possessed the consciousness that inspires a woman to present herself spiritually.

I discovered Rebbetzin Kramer through Sara Rigler (who later immortalized her in the powerful biography *Holy Woman*). When Chaya Sara was twenty, Sara told me, she was deported to Auschwitz. Her entire family was sent to the gas chambers, except for one sister who was shot dead before her eyes. Chaya Sara herself endured the worst tortures of Auschwitz, including surgery performed by the notorious Dr. Josef Mengele in his horrific medical experiments.

Yet the rebbetzin informed Sara that "Auschwitz was not a bad place."

Sara was shocked. "How can you say that?"

"I was there with a group of religious girls like me, and together we tried to keep all the mitzvot we could," Rebbetzin Chaya Sara explained. "We said blessings over food, prayed when the guards weren't watching, and kept track of the days so we'd know when it was Shabbat and try to avoid working."

They must also have performed innumerable acts of kindness to help each other stay alive.

"Where you're from," she continued, "life is good and you had everything you wanted — but there are so many Jews there who barely know what a mitzvah is. That's a bad place. For me," the rebbetzin concluded, "Auschwitz was a good place."

One can only imagine what Rebbetzin Chaya Sara looked like in Auschwitz: prisoner's rags, shaven head, emaciated. Yet even there, she focused on spiritual growth — and in struggling to perform mitzvot under the most horrible conditions, she grew tremendously. Therefore, for her, Auschwitz was a good place.

Clearly, this great woman had no need to draw attention to her body. She knew she was a soul.

Rebbetzin Chaya Sara embodies true *tzniut*. So can we.

Many of us, in our increasingly superficial society, find *tzniut* elusive. Yet if we tune into it, we can hear a still, small voice reminding us what's real. "When I see my reflection," a teenage girls muses, "sometimes I feel like I've been cheating myself [out] of something that could be mine...out of who I really am."

Tzniut is a Jewish concept, but as more people — Jews and non-Jews alike — wake up to what we all desperately need, the wisdom of Judaism's three-thousand-year-old counterculture is resonating in the mainstream.

A therapist who works with adolescent girls states: "The

most important question for every client is 'Who are you?' "

A doctor who counsels terminally ill patients writes: "We are all more than we know. Wholeness is never lost, it is only forgotten."

A young woman, sick of her friends obsessing about weight, says: "[A girl] must ask herself not *What is the size of my stomach?* but *What is the quality of my soul?*"

A leading feminist urges that we embrace a paradigm shift: "Instead of a light that is directed at us by others, a light that shines from within."

So many who have never heard the word "*tzniut*" are promoting it — under different names. For a sensitive soul understands what our world so badly needs, no matter what it's called. Our world needs people who have the courage to find themselves and let this discovery guide their lives.

Tzniut means a deep relationship with ourselves, and like any relationship, it takes time. Furthermore, in today's world, we must reaffirm this relationship daily, closing our eyes and ears to constant (and often subtle and unrecognized) messages that we're nothing more than body parts, artificial ideals are better than reality, there's only one way to be beautiful, and we should strive to be something we aren't.

Tzniut means learning to tune out the media.

4
Saying No to the Media

Jennifer recently went to a "diva" birthday party. In addition to receiving gift bags containing fashionable hair bands, she and her friends all made their own lip gloss and sparkly body gel.

Jennifer is five years old.*

Ever since Adam and Eve forfeited depth for superficiality, society has been obsessed with physicality. This obsession surrounds us — on billboards, in commercials, Internet ads, and popular magazines; and apparently even at kindergarten parties. It's the air we breathe. And we're suffering — especially females. Much more than males, females "self-objectify," evaluating themselves by outward attractiveness rather than inner qualities. And younger and younger girls

* A friend from Los Angeles reports: "That's nothing. These parties can include manicures, pedicures, even massages. And I've seen them for four-year-olds."

are requesting not only cosmetics but cosmetic surgery.

Females are likewise displaying more and more to feel good about themselves. As the body dominates our self-image, perfecting it has mushroomed from feminine preoccupation to many young women's mission in life.

Painfully, the religious Jewish world is not immune. Observant Jewish girls and women may show less skin than others, but bodies are occupying more and more of their consciousness — and *tzniut* less and less. Many are caught in a tug-of-war between the Jewish value of downplaying the body and the secular ideal of flaunting it.

The media are largely to blame.

Media-Induced Skinniness

The media rank among the most pervasive influences in the world. Mass communication is everywhere, touching nearly everyone. In the U.S. alone, advertisers spend more than $250 billion annually. Advertising is our culture — and it's fueling our body obsession. One example is "the incredible shrinking woman."

The "perfect" female featured in ads today looks (and sometimes *is*) anorexic.* Already in 2000, the typical fashion model was seven inches taller than the average woman but weighed 23% less. So much for an attainable ideal.

Yet this is the standard against which girls and women judge their bodies. In 1999, a study of fifth to twelfth grade girls discovered that while 29% were overweight, 66% wanted to lose weight. And body angst follows us into adult-

* This despite the efforts of the Dove Campaign for Real Beauty and Oprah.

hood. A *Glamour* survey found that while only one quarter of women ages eighteen to thirty-five were overweight, three quarters believed they were. Even more shocking, nearly half of all *underweight* women thought they were fat. (And that was back in 1984!) Losing ten to fifteen pounds was even more important to them than success in relationships or on the job.

Most females suffer from an extremely warped self-image, which leaves them criticizing their bodies for no reason. And *the greater their exposure to the media, the worse they feel.*

Perhaps the biggest distorters of our self-perceptions are women's magazines. Among the school students mentioned above, fashion magazine readers were far more influenced by the media's weight ideals and prone to diet. Likewise, college-age women exposed to ads featuring ultra-thin models experienced lower self-esteem, more negative moods, and greater depression than their peers — especially if the viewers were already unhappy with their bodies, as the overwhelming majority of women today are.

Television is no less insidious. The most dramatic example comes from the island of Fiji. Fijians long believed that big was beautiful. Large women were considered attractive, nobody dieted, and "You've gained weight" was a compliment. In 1995, however, television debuted in Fiji. After only three years of viewing American prime-time programs and commercials, 29% of adolescent girls were at high risk of developing an eating disorder, and 15% had made themselves vomit at least once. By 2007, 45% had thrown up in the last month. Today, eating disorders are rampant in Fiji. (For more on eating disorders, see the next chapter.)

The ideals we're fed are not only unrealistic but sometimes

even ridiculous. For many girls, the "Barbie doll" represents the feminine ideal. But how would such a thin, top-heavy figure work in real life? A computer-generated model of Barbie has shown that if she were real, her back couldn't support her upper body, leaving her to walk on all fours. More significant to the weight issue, her superskinny torso couldn't contain more than half a liver and a few centimeters of colon, resulting in chronic diarrhea. Eventually, she'd die of malnutrition. So that's the perfect body: a dead quadruped.

Yet countless little girls want to be Barbie, or at least the real-life size 2 featured in *Teen* magazine. Meanwhile, their older sisters are dying to look like the underweight *Vogue* cover girl, and their mothers like that superthin thirty-year-old model posing as a forty-five-year-old in *Good Housekeeping*. All aspire to the impossible — thanks to the media.

Marketing the Body Obsession

Weight is only part of the picture. Ultimately, the media aim to make our bodies the center of our lives. Then we'll spend more and more on them.

Advertising doesn't sell only products. It sells images and ideas, feelings and desires, dreams and values. It sells concepts of love, success, and normalcy. In short, it sells us an entire self that needs what it's advertising.

This self is externally defined. Superficial images of beautiful, thin women rewarded with fabulous lives become part of our psyches. We internalize the message that "I am my body, and perfecting and displaying it is the key to happiness." And since this self is empty, we're more likely to purchase products to fill ourselves up.

But this isn't all. Advertisers then "market inadequacy":

We're not thin enough, our stomachs aren't flat enough, our figures aren't "sculpted" enough (as if women were sculptures!), our lips aren't full enough, our hair isn't lustrous enough, our lashes aren't long enough — in other words, *we* aren't enough. While males too are vulnerable to media mantras (their "abs" aren't tight enough, their biceps don't bulge enough, etc.), females are particularly susceptible. Puberty floods a girl's brain with hormones programming her to obsess about her looks, and while this fixation will ebb, her appearance will remain a major concern. In addition, women are highly sensitive to social messages. Advertisers therefore consult psychologists, sociologists, anthropologists, behavioral scientists, etc., on how to encourage female anxiety. And they've been quite successful: Even more than two decades ago, most women were unhappy with their looks, and those deemed "pretty" were just as unhappy as those considered "plain." Female insecurity is alive and well.

Once we're dissatisfied with our all-important looks, advertisers sell us on "the core belief of American culture": Any and every physical part of us can and should be improved and upgraded, even re-created. (Indeed, the women advertising these products are themselves "re-created" to the point where their photos barely resemble their real selves.) And their products will do just that. "True beauty," the cosmetic industry tells us, "comes from within: from within bottles, jars, compacts, and tubes." Or as one author put it: "Why is it never said that the really crucial function that women serve as aspiring beauties is *to buy more things for the body*?"

In other words, the beauty industry needs you always to be "not there yet." That's why fashions change so rapidly — just when you think you're "in," you discover you're "out" and have to go shopping again. The idea is simple: If you're still trying, you're still buying.

Yet many insist they can't be so easily manipulated. "I know what advertisers are up to," they claim, "and I simply reject their messages." Easier said than done. Virtually no one can intelligently process "*all* these media images *all* the time." As stated, advertising is our culture, and no one escapes cultural influence.* Men are equally inundated. Fewer messages tell them what they should *be*, but they're told in no uncertain terms what — in terms of women — they should *want*. Many males as well insist they can differentiate between media images and real women, but associations are inescapable. Once a man has been conditioned to view only flawless, fake females as attractive, he's less likely to be drawn to an actual, imperfect one.

The beauty industry has honed "creating truths" to a fine art. Take this "fact," which virtually no one questions: Hair on a woman's legs is unattractive. An acquaintance enlightened me as to the origins of this notion. "Back in 1915, only men bought razors," she explained. "It occurred to Gillette [producer of razors] that if it could get the other half of the population to shave something, it could greatly boost

* The media have subtly manipulated not just how we look but how we live. For example, back in the '60s, the sexual revolution and the women's movement began advocating alternatives to marriage. The media quickly picked up this ball and ran with it. After all, the more isolated people are from one another, the more they spend on things they could otherwise share (Mander, *Four Arguments for the Elimination of Television*, 120). Instead of two adults buying one refrigerator, oven, and washing machine, why not promote a lifestyle in which each adult has to buy his or her own? Thus, the "glamorous single life" was born.

their income. So it started marketing a new, feminine-styled razor called Milady Decollete to American women, featuring models showing off sleek, shaven legs — and the idea caught on." And Gillette doubled its sales. Today, or course, it's not only American women, and it's not only legs. Around the world, females shave, wax, and lase hair off more and more of their bodies. A growing number of men are doing the same. All this phobic hair removal is an expensive nuisance, and my skin-cancer-conscious dermatologist says it's unhealthy, but we can't imagine not doing it. We're sold — thanks to Gillette.

Living with all this pressure to have the perfect body, it's no wonder American girls' self-esteem plummets when they hit adolescence.* To compensate them, we now have the concept of "girl power." However, as media critics have pointed out, "Almost as soon as the phrase was coined, girl power was snapped up by the media and just about everyone else was trying to sell [girls] something. What it sells is an image of being empowered. Once girls buy into that desire and go after that image, they're told that the way to get that power is through makeup, clothes and boyfriends." Listen to this blurb from a children's Web site: "Drakken and Shego are plotting a villainous scheme, and Kim Possible must save the world...again! But what is she going to wear? Take Kim on a Club Banana shopping spree to get her outfitted for her mission: who says you can't save the world and make a fashion statement at the same time!" "Girl power" is nothing more than a marketing slogan for body obsession.

---

* This plunge may also stem from brain and hormonal changes (Gurian, *The Wonder of Girls*, 20, 43).

To sum up: The beauty industry urges you to show off your body so you'll obsess about it and spend money on it. Big business wants you to be a perpetual purchaser. So we have to ask ourselves: Who do *I* want to be? Who *should* I be?

The Antidote

Thankfully, there's an antidote to the media, and virtually everyone attempting to counter their influence is promoting it. Filmmakers documenting the objectification of females in ads, feminists demonstrating outside Miss America competitions, mothers telling their teenage daughters they look more beautiful without all that makeup, therapists helping lost girls find their authentic selves — all advocate a simple yet powerful concept: *tzniut.*

Someone who knows and loves herself needn't go on display to feel valuable. Indeed, in empowering people to reclaim their self-worth, *tzniut* can spark nothing short of a personal revolution. As one teenager wisely observed, "I think the power of *tzniut* might be stronger than most kids think — I think it can reconstruct someone's entire life."

Judaism encourages women to be attractive. But true, lasting beauty combines outside and inside. For anyone capable of looking beneath the surface, *tzniut* reveals a beauty so compelling it can surprise us.

One summer here in Jerusalem, I spoke to a group of nonobservant, college-age women about *tzniut.* Afterward, one student raised her hand.

"The other night our whole program was taken to a religious wedding," she told me. "We were told to dress modestly, so we did. I took a picture of all of us there. And you know what? It's the strangest thing — we all looked so much more beautiful than usual."

Men appreciate a look that reflects what's within — at least when they're seeking a real relationship. After a young woman I know started dressing modestly, her ex-boyfriend told her she looked better than ever. In fact, a teacher in a coed Jewish high school informed me that a whole group of his students confided to him that they wished they could marry girls from the more religious school down the street.

But real beauty comes from more than just covering up. In the words of two researchers, there's something genuinely attractive about "being real to yourself and others," and some girls and women have "something special" that draws people to them. "It's not just how they look, but something deeper, like a vibe they give off, an inner something that's hard to pin down." "Being real," "something special," "something deeper," an "inner something" — could they be talking about *tzniut*?

I know a young woman who laughingly describes herself as having the kind of figure popular a few hundred years ago. She'll never be a cover girl, but her self-confidence, sparkle, warmth, and deep sense of self make her extremely attractive. Conversely, many women could be beautiful, but that "inner something" seems buried under too much makeup, desperate dieting, or other fruitless attempts to meet an artificial standard — all stemming from essential insecurity. In pursuing shallow beauty, they forfeit the real thing.

Nothing is more precious than *tzniut*. It gives us our selves and the possibility of genuine happiness. It helps protect us from superficiality and misery. And once understood, it's very hard to knock down. But it also makes us far less profitable — so the media do their best to destroy it. *Tzniut* is the media's nemesis.

"Pseudo-*Tzniut*"

To combat the media, *tzniut* must be real. Tragically, it isn't real for everyone — and as a result, the media have won over an increasing number of religious girls and women who, like their non-observant peers, no longer feel good about themselves unless their bodies are "perfect" and highly exposed.

Of course, Judaism doesn't go for body exposure. But many of us have figured out how to get around that: We just make sure our clothes are styled to emphasize certain body parts and are *tight*. To this end, we adapt secular fashions: We wear slinky, low-cut, bare-backed, spaghetti-strapped sun dresses — over high-necked, long-sleeved Lycra shirts. We go to weddings in clingy, strapless evening gowns — with body shirts underneath. Or, if more conservative, we just wear *extremely* fitted suits. We're buying into superficial, body-displaying ideals but trying to make them kosher. (More on this in Final Words: For Religious Females.) Others of us wear short skirts, violating not only the spirit of the law but the letter.

In short, we want to have our cake and eat it too, looking observant (at least technically) yet provocative. But at what cost? I was once sitting with friends in a restaurant when an Orthodox woman in her thirties walked in with her husband. She wore a short skirt, high-heeled platform shoes, a skintight top, tons of makeup, and a long curly wig cascading down her back. She clearly delighted in her husband's appreciative gaze. I later learned that she'd undergone several cosmetic surgeries, because her husband wanted a *frum* (religious) Barbie doll for a wife. I was furious at him — but I couldn't help wondering: Did she get this kind of a guy because, owing to a weak self-image, she'd presented herself as a *frum* Barbie doll since their first date?

Real *tzniut* saves us from superficiality — in our self-definition and in relationships. "Pseudo-*tzniut*" means throwing away a big part of ourselves — and very likely never being loved for who we are.

Detoxing

In summation, the media are toxic to spiritual health. They poison our self-image.

Yet it can be difficult to see this. Visiting my parents in the U.S. recently, I was taken aback at the breakneck speed at which TV commercials were flying past.

"Have commercials gotten shorter?" I asked, my head spinning.

"I don't think so," my father answered.

But of course they had. With over 100 new cable TV stations since I'd left the States, people often spend no more than a few seconds watching one channel before jumping to the next, so advertisers have to get their messages across fast. Yet my parents hadn't noticed. To them, three-second commercials were normal.

So, too, it's become "normal" for younger and younger girls to fixate on physicality and self-display. And it's now increasingly "normal" for an ostensibly religious girl to do the same. But because the change is so gradual, we don't see it for what it is. Like a frog in a kettle, who doesn't realize that the water he's in is getting hotter until he boils to death, we're oblivious to what's happening to us.

We have to recognize what "normal" is: a media ploy designed to keep us body-obsessed and buying. And we have to resist it. This means shutting out the media. We can eschew most women's magazines (which one author calls "notorious incubators of the worst of our fears and phobias"), and be highly selective in watching television (which the American Psychological Association warns is "a dominant and disturbing influence on the national psyche"). And we can seek a lifelong partner who does the same. The last thing a woman needs is a man who's viewed too many media images and wants to marry one.

In the process of weaning yourself away from the media, a wonderful thing happens: You detox.

Once I left for college, I had no TV. It's hard to describe, but as TV left my system, life felt more real. And I felt more productive and alive. Less colored by media images, I started looking at myself and others through a more natural lens, appreciating people for who they were. One young woman writes: "Sometimes I sit on a subway car and look at every woman purposefully and lovingly — as if she were my mother or best friend. It is breathtaking how beautiful they all are when I see like this." Freedom from the media makes the world look so much better.

As advertising becomes more pervasive — and invasive — it's harder to accept ourselves. My non-observant friends in the U.S. have good values, depth, and healthy self-esteem, but they can't bear the thought of aging. One was totally depressed when she turned forty. Another gets Botox injections to remove the creases in her forehead. (She once said she'd even consider a face-lift. "Why bother?" her husband joked. "I'll just find myself a younger woman." He later did.)

If we focused on the *value* of aging, we'd all be more at peace with it. Someone I know asked a roomful of middle-aged women to tell everyone their ages. They all refused. She asked, "So if you could turn back the clock twenty years, would you?" No one would. We may want to look younger, but we don't want to *be* younger. We wouldn't give up the learning and loving we've experienced for anything. Maybe we should let our appearance reflect this richness. Crow's feet mean we've smiled a lot. Gray hair signifies a long, authentic life. Why hide that?

To see beauty in an aging face, we have to detox: We must shut out the media and open up to the depths of who people are.

To see beauty, we can't sell our souls to the beauty industry.

In April 2009, forty-seven-year-old Susan Boyle appeared on the popular TV show *Britain's Got Talent*. Plump and unmade-up, unfashionably dressed and coiffed, she didn't exactly look like star material. When she said her dream was to be a professional singer, the judges looked highly skeptical. The audience looked disbelieving.

Then she opened her mouth — and blew everyone away. Initially, I thought she was lip-syncing to someone else's recording. But no: This plain-looking, middle-aged woman had a magnificent voice.

Before she'd sung even four bars, everyone was cheering. And when she finished, she received a standing ovation. People couldn't stop applauding.

They'd all written her off. And then they'd been so thrilled to be proven wrong.

Deep down, we all want to get past superficiality. We want realness. "Knowing what is real," someone wrote, "requires that we remember that we are wearing glasses, and [that we] take them off. One of the great moments in life is the moment we recognize we have them on in the first place." Susan Boyle made us realize we were wearing glasses — and when we take them off, the world is so much more beautiful. For just as anyone can have a beautiful voice, everyone can have a beautiful soul.

Tzniut enables us to tune out media messages and tune into what's real. Those who don't listen to their inner voice risk succumbing to the deadliest form of media-induced body obsession: eating disorders.

5
Ending the Hunger for Selfhood

I was told about four young couples who were enjoying a Shabbat dinner together. After dessert, one of the women noticed she was the only female left at the table. She excused herself and went to look for her friends. She found them in the hallway toward the back of the house. When she asked where they'd all disappeared to, all three nonchalantly replied that they'd gone to the bathroom to throw up, because their husbands liked them thin.

Weight control lies behind the most common eating disorders: anorexia nervosa and bulimia nervosa. No matter how skinny they are, anorexics believe they're fat, so they starve, exercise, pop diet pills, etc., until they're dangerously underweight. Bulimics overeat uncontrollably and then purge, sometimes through crash dieting or fasting and excessive exercise, but far more often through vomiting, laxatives, diuretics, or enemas.

Such people are troubled. Anorexics are often people-pleasers, attention-cravers, or perfectionists. Sometimes they're desperate to assert control over their lives. Bulimics may binge to fill an emptiness within or to numb pain, then they purge to maintain their weight. Many are stressed-out overachievers; others are depressed; yet others suffer from family dysfunction or abuse. Both anorexics and bulimics can be the simple product of inadequate mother- or father-child attachments. People with these problems should seek out a qualified therapist.*

But there's also the issue voiced by the three women above: "Our husbands like us thin."

The Cult of Thinness

Eating disorders have become a psychosociological epidemic, rooted not only in personal problems but in cultural ones affecting a particular population. Sufferers are usually from Western (or Western-influenced) countries; they develop their condition in adolescence or young adulthood; their occupations or activities often require that they be thin. And their number has snowballed within the past generation. Most significantly, nine out of ten are female. While the American Psychiatric Association reported in 2000 that as many as 8% of adolescent girls and young women struggled with anorexia or bulimia, at least one commentator states this is "just the tip of the iceberg." Aside from all the undiagnosed

---

* Eating disorders may also be a female genetic and neurological response to stress (Gurian, *The Wonder of Girls*, 214-25).

cases, an enormous number of females obsess about calories, deprive themselves of food, and feel guilty when they eat. These "mental anorexics," as they've been called, are only a hairbreadth away from real illness. According to one specialist, these cases may account for an additional 15% of adolescents.

Female appearance has always been important to both sexes. But for many young women today, it's the main source of their identity, self-expression, and self-worth. Psychologists even measure "body esteem" as a significant part of overall self-esteem, assuming that if you don't like your body, you won't like yourself.

This growing emphasis on the physical has gone hand in hand with a largely media-induced fear of excess pounds and infatuation with thinness.*

Societal pressure to be thin has changed the shape of West-

---

* Several other factors have contributed to this obsession. First, thinness is mistaken for health. Second, it's associated with restraint, moderation, and self-control, while being even slightly overweight signifies self-indulgence and inability to delay gratification — in other words, moral failure (Hesse-Biber, *Am I Thin Enough Yet?*, 4). Third, in an age of plenty and decreasing family size, plumpness no longer connotes wealth or fertility (Steinem, *Revolution from Within*, 217). Instead, we unconsciously hold the body to a machine-age standard, seeking to streamline it and eliminate anything that "slows us down or is "unnecessary" or "in the way" — like fat (Hesse-Biber, *Am I Thin Enough Yet?*, 25, citing R. P. Seid, *Never Too Thin: Why Women Are at War with Their Bodies* [New York: Prentice Hall, 1987], ch. 5). Fourth, lack of community has reduced us to strangers, making superficial criteria such as appearance an even greater priority (Pipher, *Reviving Ophelia*, 183). Finally, lack of God-consciousness has us believing we can control everything, including our own bodies.

ern beauty icons. I saw a photo of the contestants in the first Miss America pageant, held in 1921, and at least half were positively pudgy. Miss America 2008, Kirsten Haglund, was a recovering anorexic. The same trend has occurred in advertising: A 1994 Diet Rite ad featured a girl so skinny that her nickname was "Skeleton." While public pressure forced the sponsor to retract the ad, countless more have arisen in its place. Tragically, emaciated females often receive compliments on their figures right up until they're hospitalized.

Both life insurance companies and diet centers calculate ideal weights, based on height and frame. The insurance industry lists weights at which, according to medical-actuarial studies, people live longest. Diet centers list weights at which people supposedly look best. Comparing Metropolitan Life's 1983 figures with those of a major weight-loss organization, one researcher discovered a five-pound gap between the ideal weights for men, and a *twenty-pound* gap for women. In short, a woman who achieves even the 1983 cultural ideal of being twenty pounds underweight risks dying younger for it.

And she may well be willing to. A popular girls' magazine found that nearly one-third of survey respondents would rather be unhealthy than fat. In addition, two-thirds of those age eighteen to twenty-five would rather be mean or stupid, and over half would rather be run over by a truck. In fact, girls who worry they're fat are the most likely to consider or attempt suicide.

All in all, girls and women are being seduced into what has been aptly named "the Cult of Thinness." Though this cult lacks a charismatic leader, they "bow instead to powerful cultural forces that define females in terms of their physical attributes." Abiding religiously by dieting texts, they observe extensive and often fanatic food and exercise rituals in worship of the perfect body, in whose attainment they believe salvation lies.

The result of this "normative obsession" is "imitative anorexia" or "imitative bulimia" — anorexic or bulimic behavior without the underlying emotional issues. Women with this kind of disordered eating aren't disturbed; starving or purging is simply an extreme dieting strategy designed to meet society's demands on their bodies. As one psychologist states: "[Many] young women with eating disorders are not all that different from their peers. It's a matter of degree." They've simply succumbed to "culturally induced eating."

So have those who throw up because their husbands like them thin.

The Missing Self

Women with eating disorders are spiritually troubled — as are many of us. In the words of one observer: "Our dissatisfaction is never, at its deepest, about our bodies." This is what Israeli supermodel Maayan Keret discovered when she interviewed models, actresses, and dancers with eating disorders. Keret documents the frequent convergence of psychological issues with the intense pressures of a high-body-profile career, and a clear theme emerges: identification with the body and a loss of self. Loss of self means lack of self-worth and self-knowledge, detachment from one's feelings, a sense of living outside oneself, and emptiness. The body has replaced the soul. These women aren't just unhappy about their physiques — they "harbor black holes at the center of [their] beings." This is spiritual illness.

Listen to Yael, an anorexic actress: "The [real] me underneath isn't important.... I don't know what [the real me] feels — I've long ago forgotten, perhaps I never knew.... I recognize the me reflected in mirrors, display windows, photographs, films. I know her hair, her eyes...she's enough for me. The moment I feel a void...when I don't have direction and I begin to feel despair washing over me, I quickly call out, 'Stop,' and look at her. That familiar reflection is what fills me up. I have it, it's tangible, I can touch it, see it. It exists more than any thought I have in my head.... It's like an item I've bought, an item that has social and even economic value."

One off-shoot of this absent self is the need to mold oneself to others' expectations and validate the artificial "me" being projected. Listen to Jane, a bulimic model: "I felt I existed through other people, and I needed unending proof that I was worth something, and something good.... I was who I was expected to be, and it was easy for me to play the part. I didn't have to deal for a minute with what I wanted and what was good for me."

Perhaps most painful is the desperate search for love. Says Avishag, a bulimic actress: "I want to receive unending love. Unending, but my body stands in the way. It forces me to see that I'm not yet there — that I have fat."

While these women may represent the extreme, similar feelings are expressed by others who, while not in high-body-profile careers, still live in our high-body-profile society. As one anorexic girl told me, "I don't know what I have going for myself except for being really thin."

To sum up, "Young women wage war with their bodies to cope with their inner emptiness." To make peace with themselves, they must ask deep, painful, questions:

What do I want to be loved for?

Whom do I want to determine my value?

And most fundamentally:

Who am I?

Spiritual Therapy

Eating disorders are fueled by a society that has abandoned *tzniut*. When the body is central to self-definition, both psychological issues and societal expectations will play themselves out there — often resulting in obsession with thinness.

Much has been written about helping girls develop a healthy "body image." Yet the term itself is misleading. If you want a healthy body (and you should), eat right and exercise. But a healthy body *image* stems from a healthy soul. Just as you can't achieve happiness by focusing on being happy,* you can't achieve a healthy body image by focusing on your body. Whether you're overweight or anorexic, you learn to love your body not by spending hours looking in the mirror, but by loving *yourself*. I know a teenage girl who isn't skinny, but she feels and looks beautiful — because she knows *she* is beautiful.

Body image problems and eating disorders can't be treated without addressing the underlying spiritual malady. Actually, one of the most successful treatments sidesteps the disorder itself and focuses on building a sense of self. I know of a bulimic young woman who embraced *tzniut* not for

---

* Happiness occurs naturally when you appreciate what you have and listen to your soul.

religious reasons, but simply because her shaky self-esteem needed it — and she recovered. A girl is less likely to starve or purge in an attempt to achieve the "perfect self" when she knows that her "self" is much more than her body. Instilling *tzniut* is therefore essential in treating an eating disorder.

It may also be the best prevention. Research in Israel has found that religious girls have higher body satisfaction, greater self-worth, less preoccupation with food and weight, and less desire to be thin than other girls. A similar study of Jewish women in the U.S. showed that the Orthodox were less likely to be dissatisfied with their bodies or suffer from eating disorders. To be protected, however, religious women must internalize *tzniut*. Observant girls who are typically media-impacted, obsessed with physicality, and wear skintight clothing are no less prone to eating disorders than anyone else. In fact, one study conducted in a cosmopolitan area where appearance and thinness are emphasized found that Orthodox teenagers had *more* eating disorders than the general population. We must strive not only to cover what we're supposed to cover, but to know who we are.

That knowledge isn't merely intellectual, but must be part and parcel of us. Ilana Rosenblatt (of blessed memory) had it. Aside from Rebbetzin Chaya Sara Kramer (described in Chapter 3), I can think of few individuals with greater conviction than Ilana about where their true selves lie. While we may never reach this level of spiritual greatness, it can inspire.

When she was twenty-seven and a mother of four, Ilana discovered a lump. She underwent an operation, followed by chemotherapy, but the cancer had spread to her lungs, and the prognosis was poor. Yet she and her husband viewed her illness as a springboard for spiritual growth. For three years they did their utmost to increase their gratitude to and faith in God as well as their love for each other, their children, and their community.

Toward the end, Ilana was in tremendous pain, on oxygen, and constantly feeling suffocated. It could take her ten minutes to get out a sentence. Yet when asked how she was, she managed to answer:

"I wouldn't trade places with anyone."

Ilana Rosenblatt knew, with a clarity few achieve, that spiritual growth is more important than anything. Identifying herself entirely as a soul, Ilana was the exact antithesis of a person suffering from an eating disorder. If we had her conviction, we wouldn't feel empty and estranged from ourselves. We wouldn't desperately seek attention and validation.

We wouldn't throw up because our husbands like us thin.

For Parents: Raising a Healthy Daughter

A couple of generations ago, if parents were deficient or emotionally absent, society was wholesome enough that a child might still grow up with a decent sense of self. No longer, thanks largely to the media and other negative social phenomena. It is parents, therefore, who must protect their daughters from the overwhelming pressure to be thin at all costs.

If you're a mother, you are your daughter's primary female role model, and everything you say and do imprints upon her, consciously or unconsciously. From you, she'll learn if being a woman means being strong, self-confident, and happy, or insecure, people-pleasing, and unhappy. In short, she'll learn who she is and can be. When my five-year-old daughter wanted to dress like me, I suddenly realized: Everything I do or am will impact this vulnerable little person who looks up to me. It was an awe-inspiring moment.

If you're a father, your presence and involvement in your daughter's life are no less consequential to her developing self-image. You are your daughter's most powerful model of how men view women. Your thoughts and feelings about inner versus outer beauty will affect how she feels about herself.

Most important, your daughter must feel your love. Paternal support greatly boosts a girl's self-esteem and emotional well-being. I'm not talking about hugs and accolades for good grades or other accomplishments. As one author says, "All love is unconditional. Anything else is just approval." I'm also not talking about the shallow closeness that's the most some men feel comfortable offering. I'm talking about the real thing: real caring, real affection, and real connection.

At least one psychologist believes that a father's physical or (worse) emotional absence may contribute to eating disorders. His daughter may starve herself to win his approval — or at least his attention — by "achieving" a superthin body. If he's overly authoritarian, not eating may be an assertion of her autonomy. Or she may binge, trying to fill the void left by his absence. Alternately, she may do all this and more to punish herself for being unworthy of his affection, or to numb her anger at being emotionally neglected. All these reactions are cries for love rooted in "father hunger." Nearly all the women Mayan Keret interviewed were desperate for love and attention, particularly from their fathers. Make sure your daughter feels full of your love — there's no substitute for it. As one therapist states: "A father's love can make or break a girl."

Perhaps nothing can protect a daughter from a weak self-image followed by eating disorders (as well as promiscuity and other self-destructive behavior) more than knowing her parents love her for who she is. In the words of one psychologist, "Relationships are what hold girls' lives in place." Although friendships may seem to occupy center stage, a girl's relationship with her parents affects her most.* When she feels like a ship swept up in stormy seas of conflict about who she should be, the people who've known her longest and (should) know her best can be the anchor.

What about the Guys?

I have a nightmare: I have just concluded an inspiring lecture on eating disorders and *tzniut*. I have brilliantly described how society has robbed women of their true selves, how *tzniut* is the solution, and how life is not about being skinny but about loving yourself. I know the audience is sold. But there's no applause. Instead, a hundred girls and women rise to their feet, fire in their eyes. The hall reverberates, and I'm thrown backward by the force of their voices as they shout: "BUT WHO'S TELLING THIS TO THE GUYS?"

At nearly every talk I give on *tzniut*, this question is asked — by young women disgusted at what men want, or more often by mothers whose perfectly lovely but not perfectly

---

* In addition, there are huge benefits in "intergenerational mentoring" — connecting girls with women they can look up to and learn from (see Brumberg, *The Body Project*, 18–20; Gurian, *The Wonder of Girls*, 257–9).

thin daughters are still single. *You can talk about internal self-definition all you want*, they tell me, *but as long as so many males have bought into superficiality, what are we females supposed to do?*

Like women, *men have to be educated about relationships* — starting with how they should view women and what they should look for. Fathers are the primary influence here. Once they become aware of females, boys need to hear from their fathers about the qualities that make a girl truly attractive and loveable — which needn't include skinniness. Yeshivah staff too should address this issue, teaching a boy not just how to learn but how to identify the person with whom he can happily share his life. Community rabbis as well, through public and private talks, can help "graduate" a generation of single men able to really appreciate a woman. It's up to people who care to get this education off the ground. (You'll find my contribution, "Final Words: For Males," at the end of this book.)

Eating disorders, more often than not, are a disease of the soul, expressing the pain of an identity adrift. As one psychologist writes: "Girls' symptoms reflect the grief at the loss of their true selves." A woman with an eating disorder needs help figuring out who she is. She needs to feel whole. She needs *tzniut*.

We've discussed how to build a deep relationship with the right person and with yourself. Now it's time to put those ideas into practice.

PART THREE
GETTING THERE

6
Building Love

Throughout this book, I've described and illustrated the kind of loving, centered person each of us can become. This final, review chapter suggests how to get there and offers encouragement along the way. Read on, and you'll be one step closer to loving another and loving yourself.

Developing the Ability to Love

Love means appreciating goodness. We begin loving when we're drawn to another's personhood — his or her values and character, or *essence*.

Essence is what counts. Too often, however, looks, financial stability, and common interests — while important — become paramount.

To avoid this pitfall, try drafting a personal ad you'd want to answer, describing the wonderful qualities you'd want your soul mate to have. Isn't "former model" less relevant than "kindhearted"? (Attractiveness enhances a good relationship but won't do much for a bad one.) Isn't "high-earning executive" far less significant than "honest and loyal"? (Research has shown virtually no correlation between wealth and happiness.) Isn't "sailing enthusiast" immeasurably less important to lifelong love than "takes pleasure in giving," "tries to do what's right," and "wants to grow"? (A spouse can't be everything — that's why we also have friends to have fun with.) Don't deny your needs, but clarify what counts most.

Of course, you too must possess the goodness you're seeking. So ask yourself: *This wonderful person I'd love to meet — what kind of person would* he or she *want?* And realize: *I have to become that person.*

This self-growth is what makes sincerely religious young adults so impressive. While their secular peers are having "fun," they're trying to become the best people possible. Then when they finally begin dating — for marriage — they bring with them much greater self-awareness and maturity, tremendously increasing their chances of marital success. In love, they're the ones who'll win — and if you do the work, you too can be a winner.

Beyond appreciating goodness, love means focusing on the other and wanting the best for him or her. Without this orientation, we can easily confuse true love with a self-absorbed, emotional "high." How to tell the difference? Ask yourself: *If I knew this person I'm so excited about would be better off with someone else, would I hold on or let go?*

My friend Joy told me that, early in her marriage, she had a very difficult Elul. (Elul is the month preceding Rosh

HaShanah, the Jewish New Year, when we take stock of ourselves and examine where we need to grow.) After deep introspection, she reached the disheartening conclusion that she was a spiritual zero, her husband had made a terrible mistake in marrying her, and he should divorce her and find someone better. Although her husband lovingly rejected this idea, Joy was miserable. But one thing consoled her: If she thought her husband should divorce her, she couldn't be such a failure, because at least she really loved him.

We all want to marry quality people. It's therefore wise to have a trusted acquaintance prescreen your dates. Alternately, here's a suggestion: Invite anyone interested in you to join you in volunteering. If the person accepts, he or she is probably worth getting to know. (And you can always spend time together afterwards, just the two of you.) Use your own creativity to come up with other ideas about how to "sift out" higher-quality dates.

Beyond essence and spiritual compatibility, looks are important. Unfortunately, they can blind us. Attraction can inflate even the slightest positive quality while whitewashing glaring flaws. How to gain clarity? Imagine the object of your affections being downright homely. Is he or she still as impressive? And as the relationship progresses, continually ask yourself: *Despite my date's attractiveness, can I see real shortcomings in him or her?* When you're in danger of being carried away by looks, frequent reality checks can keep you grounded.

Distinct un-attraction, on the other hand, can distort in the opposite direction, causing us to exaggerate faults while overlooking virtues. If you're not initially attracted, picture the other person as very good-looking, and ask yourself how his or her words and deeds come across now.

In general, when you meet someone new, experiment with your "vision." Try to erase all preconceptions ("she should be gorgeous," "he should exude confidence and success") and see the other as is. Or try looking at the person as if he or she were a good friend. Can that funny-looking nose be cute? Can that awkward shyness be endearing? Don't lose objectivity about character and values, but in the realm of attraction, try on the subjective view you'll want after marriage, and see if the other person becomes more appealing.

Another thing you can "try on" when a relationship starts getting serious is the feeling of oneness — that your destinies, happiness, and very souls are bound together. If you say something hurtful to the other person, imagine it boomeranging. Even more powerfully, imagine your right hand cutting your left. It's hard — but it's good preparation for the spiritual reality of marriage.

The Power of Not Touching

One of the most important steps you can take to achieve genuine love is being *shomer negiah*. Few practices are as potentially life-changing. One American graduate student in psychology called it "brilliant," and countless others can personally attest to its power — or will at least admit the idea makes a lot of sense. Being *shomer negiah* causes you to see the other person more clearly and deeply.

Yes, it's hard — but not as hard as society would have you believe.

Those of us who grew up secular were taught not to expect too much of ourselves — and particularly not of males. Even upon becoming religious, this cynicism can be hard to shake. My friend Debbie realized as much when, shortly after marrying, she challenged her husband Jon. "Don't tell me the guys you know make it until marriage without fooling around."

To her amazement, Jon was insulted. "Do you really think we men are such babies?" he asked. "If guys hang out with girls, post pictures of women on their dormitory walls, and watch certain movies, it's probably very hard. But my friends don't. They avoid temptation. Besides, most of the time they're studying, working, or volunteering, and in their free time they do healthy things they enjoy, like sports, hiking, or traveling.

"A guy can make life easy or hard for himself. If we want to, believe it or not, we can control ourselves."

In other words, whether you're male or female, *don't underestimate yourself.* If you structure your life intelligently, you'll be surprised what you can do, and with no great suffering. You're stronger than you think.

If you're still doubtful, think of other challenges you'd meet for the sake of future reward. Can you imagine passing up pizza and ice cream to achieve a healthy weight? Working in a tedious job to earn enough to buy a car? Spending most of your time studying in pursuit of your dream career? Being *shomer negiah* is no different: It's all about delaying gratification. Undeniably, physical relationships are a big gratification to delay, but if you're serious about getting the most out of life, you'll hold off — and you'll reap the benefits.

Besides fortifying yourself ideologically, take practical precautions. You're far more likely to remain *shomer negiah* if your get-togethers take place in a religious rather than secular milieu, or in broad daylight downtown rather than on an isolated park bench at two in the morning.

But don't humans need touch? Humans need what touch produces: oxytocin. Not only does oxytocin makes us feel connected and happy, but it relieves stress and promotes healing.

Fortunately, male-female involvement isn't the only source of oxytocin. Ask for a hug, a massage, or other affectionate contact from same-sex friends, siblings, parents, or anyone else you feel comfortable with. (I suspect this piece of advice is more relevant to girls than to guys.) It's not the same as being married, but it can take the edge off any frustration while you're waiting.

Even altruism can release oxytocin — so try running errands for someone housebound, helping a pregnant woman carry her groceries, or shoveling snow from an elderly neighbor's sidewalk. Combining physical contact *and* altruism is especially effective: Care for a handicapped person, a baby, or even a pet. Not only will you enjoy that warm, connected feeling, but your life will be much richer. (Even the smallest good deed can create a wonderful "helper's high." I remember getting an incredible one just from taking a couple of suitcases off an airport carousel for a man with a back problem.)

Loneliness can reflect a craving for oxytocin — but fortunately, socializing too can cause an oxytocin response. Phone or get together with a good friend or develop your social networks. Again, combining sociability with generosity — such as through group volunteer work — will increase its effect.

Of course, seeking a chemical boost isn't the only reason to be caring and productive. *Chessed* (loving-kindness) will also make you a more giving and thus a better human being and future spouse. In general, these pre-marriage years are when you should be working on becoming worthy of marrying someone amazing — and *chessed* tops the list of growth-producing activities.

If you're male, do an important *chessed* for yourself as well: Decide how you want to relate to women. Remember that your outer will pulls you away from your deepest needs and desires, while your inner will directs you to fulfill them. When you're with a female, ask yourself: *Which will is she activating?* Focus on your inner will. And if that means removing yourself from her company, you're doing *her* a favor too. Women can really lose their heads in a relationship and then suffer when it's over. Don't put them in this position. Don't leave them with painful memories.

If you're female, ask yourself what will *you're* activating in the male you're with. If the outer, you're impeding his spiritual growth. Wouldn't you rather assist it? There's no greater *chessed* than helping another human being actualize his spiritual potential.

Whether male or female, if you feel yourself wavering, remember: However much we need physicality, *we need love more* — and refraining from physical contact while dating will help you get the real thing.

Once you're engaged, restraining yourself can be even more difficult. Remember that beyond the practical benefits of being *shomer negiah*, there's something called *holiness*. Imagine touching for the first time as husband and wife, knowing you're expressing not just a feeling but a lifelong commitment. If necessary, don't see too much of each other before the wedding. It may be challenging, but you've come this far, so stick it out and go for the gold. You'll be glad you did.

At the same time, think creatively about how you can express your feelings nonphysically. Flowers? A poem? (As wonderful as physicality is, words can be even more powerful.) A picture? Cookies? (I've got a great recipe for carob-sunflower-seed-raisin-oatmeal cookies if he or she is too health-conscious for chocolate chip.) Little things like this can touch the heart.

All in all, remember: *Being* shomer negiah *is the acid test.* When you're getting to know one another, it's the acid test of sincerity: *Are we interested in each other not for what we can get, but for who each other genuinely is?* When you're emotionally involved, it's the acid test of strength: *Although it's getting hard, can we keep deepening our relationship?* And when you're engaged, it's the acid test of spirituality: *Is our relationship holy?*

Sincerity, strength, and spirituality. All these can be the hallmarks of your dating relationships — if you're *shomer negiah.*

Living from Your Core

Healthy love for another requires healthy love for yourself — and *tzniut* helps you get there. *Tzniut* means defining yourself as a soul, the most inherent — and inherently lovable — part of you. Your appearance and conduct shouldn't dominate your self-image; they should reflect it.

Sometimes people tell me they don't know who they are inside — which can make the whole concept of *tzniut* perplexing. As one girl put it: "I don't really understand what it means to have my 'outer self' reflect my 'inner self.' If I don't know who I am, how could I be 'in touch with my soul'?"

"Finding yourself" is beyond the scope of this book, and

if the issue troubles you, you may need help, even from a professional. But you can start by trying to differentiate between what you think others expect of you and what you want for yourself. Ask yourself: *What do* I *like? What makes* me *happy?* Then find healthy ways to bring those things into your life: colors, objects, food, activities, education, places, people, or anything else that affirms *you*. Eventually, you'll want to work up to far more important concerns: *What makes me feel spiritually contributive? In what ways can my goodness manifest itself?*

Once your self-image is more solid, *tzniut* will strengthen it.

While *tzniut* far transcends what we wear, dress is significant in forming our sense of self. Unconsciously, we tend to see ourselves partially as we believe others do. This means we can alter our self-image by wearing clothes that elicit the feedback we want. For example, I dress more formally for formal presentations and less formally for informal ones. How I'm perceived and therefore perceive myself affects my language and demeanor, and thus my ability to reach my audience.

A college student I know experimented with this idea one day by wearing a long, loose skirt instead of her usual tight pants. "Men treated me more respectfully, and I liked it," she told me.

Test out the power of the "looking-glass self" yourself: Dress differently than you usually do, and note how differently others respond to you — and how differently you *feel*. Then you'll realize how much of your self-image is within your control.

A healthy self-image means, among other things, not

needing superficial attention. Quality attracts quality, so present yourself more substantively. You don't need the approval of someone with little or no regard for the real you. As a woman I know said of some unsavory coworkers, "It's a compliment *not* to get attention from guys like that!" That's someone who believes in herself — as we all should.

To test how solid you are and where you may need to grow, periodically "check your messages." What are you broadcasting? (Be honest.) If the message is mixed — such as "Don't notice me, but notice me" — identify which part you really want. Then come up with several statements of affirmation that you can repeat to yourself when challenged (such as "My self-worth is independent of how anyone looks at me").

Another way to develop a more internal self-image is to heighten your appreciation of privacy. Don't reveal every aspect of your life to just anyone who comes along. And when conversing in public, lower your voice to remind yourself that your conversation — like your body — isn't for public consumption. Remember: Privacy doesn't mean stuffiness; it means reserving parts of yourself for those with whom it's appropriate to share.

A mother can have immeasurable impact on her daughter's developing self-image. One way to teach real, internal *tzniut* is through praise. I was taught that parents should offer at least five times as much praise as criticism, and to that I'll add that they should praise inner qualities — such as generosity, caring, good judgment, and maturity — at least ten times as often as appearance. And when they do admire their daughter's looks, they should connect them to her inner self.

I once walked into a neighbor's home and saw a pretty little girl, perhaps ten years old, sitting in the living room. "This is Rachel," my neighbor introduced her daughter. "Isn't she cute?" I winced. *I'll bet everyone calls her cute*, I thought, *and she thinks that's her identity*. But then the mother added, "It must be because of all the mitzvot she does." The girl's initial uncomfortable smile turned into a glow.

All it takes is a little creativity to link appearance to something deeper. A grandmother told me that when she was little, she asked her mother, "Am I pretty?" Her mother replied, "Pretty is as pretty does" — that is, you're as beautiful as your deeds. Of course, this doesn't mean a mother can't compliment her daughter's looks. But when a girl comes out of her room in a nice, new outfit, instead of saying only, "You look so pretty!" Mom can add, "Inside and out."

My thirteen-year-old daughter came home from the park one day all excited. "I made a new friend!" she announced.

"Wonderful!" I congratulated her. "How did it happen?"

"We just started talking. Actually, she did. She came over and said, 'Something about you is so pretty.' "

A bell went off in my head: *Aha — a golden opportunity to instill* tzniut.

"Did she say it was your eyes?" I asked innocently.

"No."

"Your hair?"

"No."

"Your dress?"

She shook her head. "She just said, 'Something about you.' "

"Well," I said, smiling, "it sounds like she means something deeper, like who you are inside, which shines out. I think she's talking about your *neshamah* [soul] — because that makes you more beautiful than anything else."

Of course, a parent's praise must be age-appropriate. Telling your teenage daughter she looks like a *bat Melech* (daughter of the King) may not work, since most teenagers no longer want to be "princesses." They want to look "in." Unfortunately, their hopelessly "out of it" mothers can't very well reassure them. So try something like: "I bet your friends think that outfit is perfect for you! It really brings out who you are."

One problem girls struggle with is societal dress codes. *Tzniut* is sometimes equated with a specific look. Girls who dislike that look may conclude, "Well, since I've abandoned *tzniut* by wearing a faded denim skirt, I may as well wear a tight shirt too." *Wrong.* A faded denim skirt may be inappropriate for certain circles, but unless it's too short or snug, it doesn't contradict *tzniut*, whereas a tight shirt does. While *tzniut* means presenting yourself as a person, there are many kinds of people in the world. You can be who you want and still dress with *tzniut*.

Tzniut is also crucial in interactions. "Social *tzniut*" — creating appropriate boundaries — helps define personhood. Unclear boundaries — confusion about what should be shared and what shouldn't — are rampant today, especially among females. A person who doesn't know where she ends and the next person begins will have trouble deeply knowing herself.

Boundaries are especially important in the workplace, where many of us spend most of our waking hours and where inappropriate relationships can most easily develop. If you suspect you may be too buddy-buddy with an opposite-sex boss or coworker, ask yourself: *How can I be friendly yet draw a clear line between us?* Remember that most inappropriate relationships start innocently. You needn't stop smiling — but be more formal in your appearance, speech, and behavior. Dress a bit more modestly, such as by buttoning another button. If you're female, wear less makeup; look your best for your husband (or date), not for your boss. Male or female, rather than contact lenses, wear glasses, which can subtly increase psychological distance between people. Avoid chitchat. If possible, refer to people by title and last name. Resist prolonged eye contact and the subtle intimacy it sometimes creates. If you're married and the conversation gets personal, mention your spouse and children. Keep a conspicuous picture of them on your desk. All in all, by not putting so much of yourself "out there," you strengthen what's "in here," keeping intimacy where it belongs. Exercising reserve with members of the opposite sex expresses emotional fidelity to, and love for, that special person with whom you *are* (or will someday be) bonded.

Tzniut in dress is also a form of reserve — and here, as in being *shomer negiah*, women can do men a great service. If you're female, be sensitive to the impact of your attire on males. Ask yourself: *Is what I'm wearing making life easier or harder for guys?* Work on surpassing the need for ego-gratifying attention, and care about others (and their wives). Remember: You don't need to be noticed by the wrong people — you need to be *seen* by the right ones.

If you're male, another way of exercising reserve is *shmirat einayim*. While you can't control what's on the street, *you* can control where you look. When you see a provocatively dressed female, think of looking away as a gift of love to yourself and your wife (or future wife).

Above all, *tzniut* means remembering who you really are. Dr. Rahamim Melamed-Cohen isn't likely to forget. A leading figure in special education in Israel, he was diagnosed at age fifty-seven with Lou Gehrig's Disease (ALS), which gradually paralyzes the body, ending with the lungs. Now in the final stages of this deadly illness, he is unable to speak and on life support. Nevertheless, the last I heard, he was still attending synagogue, studying Torah, and administering a small yeshivah. And via a computer controlled by eye movements, he has composed poetry, artwork, and — most important — numerous books intended to help others. He also corresponds with countless people desperate for his wisdom and encouragement.

When interviewed, what did Dr. Melamed-Cohen have to say about his existence?

"These are the best years of my life."

Think of the wonderful things this amazing man is doing, and the deep satisfaction and joy he must feel — because he defines himself as a soul.

Needless to say, we'd like to reach the level of these exceptional individuals without undergoing their trials. So ask yourself: *If I were severely handicapped, how could I nonetheless illuminate the world?*

Don't wait for your life to be turned upside down to realize who you are and what you have to give. Let your vision of your potential self be your own guiding light.

Negating the Media's Influence

The media and the beauty industry want us to define ourselves superficially, focus on our physical imperfections, dislike ourselves, and then buy things to make ourselves feel better. In other words, they manipulate us to our detriment and their benefit — and our very souls are at stake.

Should we accept this treatment — or resist?

Personally, I strive to be as non-profitable as possible. The less money I put into the beauty industry's coffers, I figure, the healthier and more centered I am.

This doesn't mean one shouldn't care about his or her appearance. Most of us, especially women, need to feel attractive. Yet this need must be balanced with healthy self-acceptance. There's a difference between spending a moderate amount of time and money to look your best and spending your life (and life savings) trying to look like some media image you can't possibly recreate.

So, to answer my own question, I advocate active resistance to the media: Consider seriously cutting down on — or, ideally, cutting out — much of popular music, magazines, television, and movies. Declare a one-month "media detox." During this period, spend as much time as possible engaged in meaningful activities with real people. It may be difficult at first to wean yourself off your addiction. But just as eating whole foods makes you physically healthier, looking at and doing only wholesome things will make you spiritually healthier. Gradually, you'll see the world and the people in it — including yourself — more genuinely. You'll feel cleaner. After one month, you can reevaluate the media's place in your life.

The only way to avoid media influence is to avoid the media. If you can't, at least deglamorize their images by training yourself to critique them. When you see a seductive ad, be skeptical. Realize that, in most cases, you're being encouraged to look like someone whose picture has been airbrushed to perfection. I remember reading about a model whose magazine photos were so digitally altered that she said she wouldn't even recognize herself if not for the mole on her cheek. A Los Angeles friend tells me that out-of-towners used to seeing celebrities only in magazines often can't identify them on the street, as their real selves bear no resemblance to their Photoshopped incarnations. Other publications go further, "constructing" people who are composites of many individuals. One magazine cover featured a face composed of five blended images. Such "people" simply don't exist. And if they did, given the toll self-display takes on self-image, they'd probably be unhappy (as many celebrities indeed are).

Aside from deconstructing media images, reconstruct real people. Rather than measuring them against artificial ideals, practice seeing their deeper, true, unique beauty. Then try looking in the mirror, as long as necessary, until you see your own.

Along with imbuing yourself with internal *tzniut*, stand firm about how you want to present yourself. After visiting a few supermarkets and finding only questionable *hechsherim* (kashrut certifications), you wouldn't shrug and say, "Well, what can I do? I'm sure some people would rely on the rabbinate of North Korea." So don't wimp out on external *tzniut* either. Go into as many stores and try on as many things as you have to, check out as many Internet sites as necessary, or even have something custom-made — but *don't compromise your integrity.* Make sure your clothing expresses your highest self.

Remember: Every day you resist the media's influence and dress with *tzniut*, you're telling them — and yourself — that your criteria, not theirs, determine your self-worth.

You're winning the war for your soul.

And don't forget to ask for help from the One Above. As one girl prays: "God, let me see [myself] through Your eyes and not the world's."

Feeling Full Inside

Eating disorders have skyrocketed in recent years. While their causes are often psychological (and/or possibly genetic or neurological), a salient one is spiritual: estrangement from oneself. *Tzniut*, therefore, must be part of the cure — and the prevention.

Start by finding out your medically ideal weight. It will be heavier than what popular media portray. Remind yourself that this is what you're *supposed* to weigh (and that, at this weight, you would have been considered most attractive not so long ago). If you weigh significantly less, you may be shortening your life and/or compromising your health. Consult with a nutritionist to come up with a diet that will help you reach your ideal weight. Be honest and realistic, and shoot for healthy and happy.

More importantly, remember that you're not a number on a scale. Your value can't be quantified, and certainly not in pounds and ounces (or kilos). It lies in how good a person you are. The size of your body has no bearing on the quality of your soul.

Believe it or not, some young women would rather be dead than fat. If you're one of them — and overweight — imagine hearing about a neglected, unhappy girl desperate for love and attention. She's in danger of sliding into self-destructive behavior, such as promiscuity and drug use. Taking this girl under your wing, you could turn her life around.

Would you still rather be dead?

Just as you can probably think of someone (who may even have been fat) without whom your life would not be the same, there are people hungry for what you can give. (And if you're an emotional eater, giving can fill that empty space you might otherwise stuff with food.) *Never undervalue your life.*

Knowing your worth should propel you toward spiritual growth, which will in turn promote deeper self-love and happiness. It's been found that religious involvement (which should include Torah study) and community participation improves mental well-being. Specifically, prayer and other religious rituals boost self-esteem, empowerment, and contentment. And don't forget the quintessential spiritual act: *chessed*. It takes you out of yourself, makes you feel great, and builds self-worth as you see yourself enhancing others' lives. It's the closest thing to a spiritual cure-all there is.

If you're a mother, you have a phenomenal opportunity to steer your daughter toward spirituality — or the opposite. Your daughter's feelings about herself and her body start with you. Are you obsessed with your appearance? Does she hear you complaining about your figure? Does she see you looking at yourself critically in the mirror? Does she witness you engaging in unhealthy eating? Body dissatisfaction, where most eating disorders begin, is contagious, and girls contract it not only from their peers but particularly from their mothers. If, on the other hand, your daughter sees you're at peace with your appearance and happy with yourself as a person, you're sending her a priceless message about what womanhood should be.

If you're a father, don't give your daughter the impression that only thin women are attractive, or that looks are the most important thing in a relationship — you'll be putting her at significantly higher risk of developing an eating disorder. Let her know that different women are beautiful in different ways, that character and personality greatly color looks, and that even physical "imperfections" can be appealing. (Would singer-actress Barbra Streisand be half as attractive if she'd had her nosed "fixed"?) Show her that you value substance in a woman. One fifteen-year-old recalls her divorced father's describing a woman he dated as smart and funny, mentioning only afterwards that she was beautiful, and even then, "not in a conventional way." This depiction taught the daughter a lot about the role of appearance in a relationship and the power of inner beauty.

In many other ways, parents can help their daughters develop a healthy self-image and a healthy attitude toward food and weight. Don't use food to reward or punish. Don't use the word "diet" — just talk about eating right. Compliment people's inner qualities, and when you do compliment their physical selves, stress things such as strength, athletic ability, or agility as opposed to looks. And teach your daughter to appreciate diversity — that beauty comes in all sizes and shapes, and at all ages.

Most of all, give your daughter positive messages about herself.

My friend Shoshanna's slightly chubby pre-teen asked her, "Mommy, am I fat?"

Shoshanna could have replied, "Fat? Of course not! Just because you're not skinny doesn't mean you're fat!" Not a bad answer, but it still centers on weight. Instead, she sidestepped the question and changed the focus. "You know what I see when I look at you?" Shoshanna said. "I see your *neshamah* sparkling in your eyes, and that makes every inch of you beautiful."

But what if your daughter says, "You didn't answer my question — so you think I *am* fat?" And what if she *is*? Again, instead of focusing on weight, emphasize effort and intention, and link outside to inside. As one wise mother answered her daughter:

"We all have to work on ourselves in two ways: We have to eat right and exercise in order to have healthy bodies — and a healthy body won't be exactly the same for everyone. We also have to work on our relationships with others and with God in order to have healthy souls — and a healthy soul also won't be exactly the same for everyone. While it would be good for you to lose some weight, I feel blessed and proud to have a daughter who works hard on both parts of herself — and that makes you beautiful, inside and out."

Imagine a society in which love of oneself and of others comes naturally. People know who they are and what they have to give and instinctively look for the same goodness in another. Upon finding the right person, they relate deeply, and because they connect on the level of essence, their love endures.

Sound like a dream? It needn't be. With education and commitment, we can make it reality. We can learn how to genuinely bond with ourselves and others. God gave us all the ability; we just have to recognize and use it. And we'll be so grateful we did — for nothing brings greater joy than choosing to love.

Final Words

A great deal of this book has dealt with the female challenge of defining and presenting ourselves holistically. I've also spoken about the male challenge of relating to women spiritually. These practices underlie the very health of our self-images, relationships, and societies. With so much at stake, I offer some of my strongest statements in the following final words.

For Religious Females

Torah is an amazing gift from God. Even rote observance of Torah ethics guarantees we'll be decent people living decent lives. And if we broaden our observance and invest it with spirituality, we're guaranteed to be exceptional people living exceptional lives. But to reach that level, we have to work on ourselves.

This principle is especially true in *tzniut*. Tuning in to the spiritual dimension of *tzniut* requires awareness and effort. While many succeed beautifully, for some, it's a struggle.

As I've said, *tzniut* is not a dress code. And its purpose is not to make you look frumpy or nerdy. *Tzniut* is a sense of self and a way of being that speaks volumes about what you believe in and value. Its purpose is to deepen and transform you, allowing you to project a genuine, holistic beauty and to love yourself and be loved for who you are. Anything less makes *tzniut* a farce.

Of course, we don't have to care about lofty ideals or the spirit of the law. We can just make sure we're minimally, bottom-line observant, doing whatever we want as long as it's not technically forbidden.

In my early years of observance, I was privileged to know only wonderful, sincerely religious people, never encountering this kind of Judaism. But I finally did — after a bad date. The young man and I hadn't been so comfortable at our first meeting, so he thought doing something "normal" next time might help. He suggested going to a "kosher" movie recommended by a friend in his yeshivah. I didn't argue, although going to a movie — as opposed to getting to know one another — wasn't my idea of a *frum* date.

Well, that also wasn't my idea of a kosher movie. After the third nonkosher scene, I said, "I don't know about you, but I'm leaving," to which he quickly replied, "Me too."

I was very bothered by this whole incident — especially since he himself hadn't suggested leaving. I called a rabbi at his yeshivah and told him (without mentioning names) what had happened. "What's your yeshivah's attitude toward movies," I asked, "and particularly ones like this?"

"We don't expect our students not to go to movies," he told me. "And if the one you went to showed nothing explicit, it's not *assur* [forbidden]." Oh. It *implied* things that would have been *assur* to see had they been explicit. It degraded women. It was offensive and disgusting. But not *assur*. So no problem.

"Not *assur*" *tzniut* is unfortunately not unheard of in some communities. A girl will say to me, "What does it matter if my shirt is snug and emphasizes my chest? If it covers what it's supposed to cover, it's not *assur*." Or "So what if when my shirt comes up, you see my underwear? If it's not my skin, it's not *assur*." Or "What difference does it make if my long wig is so natural-looking and attention-getting that a guy thought I was single and started up with me? If it's not my real hair, it's not *assur*." (The truth is, it would be hard to find a rabbi who would agree that dressing this way — or seeing the movie I was taken to — is in fact not *assur*.)

We may be blind to what we're doing, but outsiders often aren't, and sometimes they call us on it. *National Geographic* once featured a photo essay on a particular group of American Orthodox Jews. At the end of the magazine, the photojournalist — a non-Jewish woman — talked about the assignment. She recounted how she'd been advised to enter the community dressed modestly, so she wore a loose T-shirt and baggy jeans. "But apparently they define modesty differently," she said, "because the women were all wearing form-fitting skirts."

Ouch.

The Judaism I was taught and came to love isn't a non-thinking, "do the minimum and get away with it" religion. It's about introspection and growth, about developing meaningful relationships with God, others, and ourselves. That doesn't mean we have to be existential philosophers. But we do have to be honest.

One thing we have to be honest about is the meaning of "tight." A girl I know once asked me how she looked, and I commented that her shirt was tight. "It is?" she asked, surprised.

I was surprised at her surprise. "It's the exact same size as your body," I pointed out. "It's 'form-fitting.' Isn't that called tight?"

She shook her head. "Tight is when the shirt is *smaller* than your body and has to stretch to fit around it."

To eliminate such disagreements, maybe we should adopt an objective definition one rabbi has proposed: "Tight" means your clothing's circumference is less than four inches (ten centimeters) greater than that of your body. If your bust is thirty-five inches, your shirt should measure thirty-nine inches around. This means you should be able to "pinch" two inches of material (*without* stretching it) at the side.

Yet I dislike the "tape measure" approach to *tzniut.* I prefer sensitivities to centimeters. Fortunately, there's another quick and easy way to see if you're being honest with yourself about *tzniut.* Put on whatever you want to wear, close your eyes, and walk to a full-length mirror. Now open your eyes and see where they go — because that's where other eyes will go too. If your gaze fixes on a certain body part, something's probably too tight — and that's what people will notice about you. If your eyes appreciate your appearance yet come to rest on your face, you're attractively dressed *and* your personhood is coming through.

Before buying a questionable article of clothing, tight

or not, be honest about why you like it. If it's designed to be revealing and provocative, no matter how many layers you put underneath, ask: *Is it for me?* Or you can ask: *The woman I respect the most in the world* (name her) — *would she be happy to see me in this? Would she feel it reflects who I am?* Finally, if you realize the outfit isn't for you, ask: *Is there something else I can buy in which I'll look not like a beautiful body, but like a beautiful* person — *inside and out?*

Embracing *tzniut* requires belief in yourself — which doesn't come easily to many of us. "I want to dress with true *tzniut*," a sincere young woman told me, "but there's so much pressure not to. These days, even some students in the best yeshivahs want an eye-catching wife to show off to their friends. If I don't dress at least a little provocatively, I won't get a really good guy."

Excuse me: I don't care how large a guy's *kippah* (yarmulke) is, or how prestigious his yeshivah. If he wants to be seen with a "hot" wife, he's *not* a "really good guy." He may wear the uniform and do what he's supposed to do, but he's as media-influenced and spiritually compromised as any secular male on the street. If a girl wants a *genuinely* good guy, she herself may have to get past externals and seek someone whose religiosity is through-and-through.

Developing genuine spirituality is, it seems, the challenge of our generation. Given the proliferation of religious communities, observing Shabbat and the holidays needn't be difficult; the abundance of kosher products lining the supermarket shelves makes kashrut a breeze; synagogues are attractive and air-conditioned; and the local *mikveh* (pool for ritual immersion) is often modern, spotless, and even luxurious. Arguably, anyone who wants to can be technically "observant" without huge effort or sacrifice. But if someone wants more — to become closer to God; to be a better, more spiritual person; and to attain a truly, deeply loving relationship with her spouse and with herself — she must *do* more. She must look to her core, constantly questioning, challenging herself, and striving to grow. And nothing touches that core more than *tzniut*.

For All Males

Guys, I know how important physical attraction is to you. God hardwired your brains to be visual. At the same time, all those stereotypical media images of skinny, gorgeous women can create a very narrow, artificial definition of beauty. You may consequently find it difficult to date someone who isn't a knockout. But give a girl a chance — not for her sake, but for *yours*.

Deep, lasting attraction far transcends physical appeal: It's a potent product not only of looks, but also of chemistry, personality, and character. It's highly individual. And the more it stems not only from appearance but from who a person is inside, the more powerful and enduring it is.

Females often understand this truth more easily. "I've dated some exceptional-looking guys," a woman told me. "But many had little substance, so they became less attractive to me. On the other hand, I've dated guys (including my husband) who I thought were nice-looking but not 'gorgeous.' But with time, their character, inner strength, and intelligence made them 'gorgeous' to me. When I first started dating my husband, all my girlfriends said, 'He doesn't look anything like the guys you usually date.' Now they say, 'I wish I had a husband like yours.' "

While this phenomenon of someone "growing on you" is more common to women, it can happen to men as well. Andy was a stereotypical "jock," unaccustomed to deep relationships with women. Then he met a friendly, intelligent young woman named Deborah at the front desk of a Jewish organization.* He had some questions about Judaism, and they ended up talking awhile. Although her looks didn't do much for him, her mind and personality impressed him. They spoke more the next day, and the day after, and the day after that. After two weeks of increasingly deep and personal conversation, he was blown away. Never had he felt so much for someone — and now he was crazy about her looks as well.

Josh had a similar experience: "I've always liked beautiful, thin, dark-skinned, exotic girls. Then I met Tammi — a nice-looking, medium-weight, fair-skinned American. But she was fun, bubbly, and outgoing. Most of all, I loved her realness. She was so comfortable with who she was — she had no need to put on a show. I felt I could become her best friend. And the more I got to know her, the more I was physically attracted to her. Now we're engaged. I think she's beautiful, but it's not only about the surface — it's about the whole 'package.' She's awesome."

David, too, met a girl who was "okay-looking but nothing special," "not my type," and someone who "if I saw her on the street, I wouldn't look twice." At the same time, she was bright, idealistic, and caring, all of which he was drawn to. At his rabbi's urging, he agreed to give the relationship a

---

* This story is recounted at greater length in *The Magic Touch.*

try. Sure enough, over the next few weeks she began looking better to him — but still he wasn't feeling the attraction he wanted. Then, on their next date, he lost his glasses. And he realized: *God is sending me a message to look at her differently.* He made a final effort to drop all preconceptions about what she "should" look like — and suddenly, her attractiveness grew. Before long, they were engaged. After the wedding, he told me he couldn't get over how beautiful she was. And two decades later, he feels the same way.

Just as *tzniut* is best understood not intellectually but experientially, so too with "letting someone grow on you." Give yourself a chance to experience it. Upon meeting a woman, don't rush to figure out whether you're attracted enough to marry her. At the end of the date, just ask yourself, "Would I enjoy seeing her again?" If so, and if you continue going out, you may have the powerful experience that Andy, Josh, David, and countless other happily married men have had. And you may end up a changed person. As one author notes, "the act of seeing can transform the person who sees and cause us to see differently for the rest of our lives."

While stereotypically beautiful women can also have wonderful qualities, they often have less impetus to develop them. To quote a friend and onetime model: "As victims of a society focused on externals, beautiful women face a greater challenge to self-development. As children, adults indulge them more than their less attractive friends. As they grow older, they automatically get better service, and men are more interested in them. The result can be low self-esteem, shallowness, or even self-centeredness and a tendency to manipulate. And because they're often addicted to the kind of attention their beauty attracts, after marriage they may become unhappy and demanding, or resort to flirting with other men to regain their self-worth. Sadly, good looks can corrupt what could otherwise be an attractive personality."*

Externally self-defined women are also more likely to spend an inordinate amount of time on their looks. Nothing's wrong with an occasional manicure, pedicure, or professional hair styling. But when appearance becomes an obsession — complete with *constant* calorie-counting and exercise — there's much less time for more spiritual or other-oriented pursuits (particularly when recuperating from cosmetic surgery). While women should look nice — especially for their husbands — doing so shouldn't preclude other important things in life, like spiritual growth.

More significantly, immediate attraction based primarily on externals can be misleading. As Josh puts it: "When I'd go out with a woman I immediately found beautiful, I'd lose all clarity. I'd try to make everything work around the fact that I was attracted to her." If you're smitten by looks, you're more prone to sweep any flaws under the rug. But they'll crawl out after marriage — and you may realize you've made a terrible mistake. (This doesn't mean you shouldn't date someone you're immediately attracted to — just hang onto your critical faculties.)

Gradual, "whole person" attraction, on the other hand, has distinct advantages. It gives you a far greater chance of marrying the right woman for the right reasons. Rooted in qualities deeper than looks, this attraction will more likely be

* Thankfully, due to the emphasis on character development and gender separation, most pretty girls in my community have not suffered this fate.

alive and well thirty years from now, despite any "wear and tear," weight gain, or pregnancy-related bodily changes your wife may undergo. And the attraction will be of the singular sort with which other women can't compete. There's no better recipe for keeping love alive.

In short: When a woman's looks color your perception of her character and personality, you're apt to end up with the wrong person and fading attraction; when her character and personality color your perception of her looks, you're in for lifelong love.

Aside from all the pitfalls of an attraction-based relationship, the unnatural skinniness often considered attractive today can be downright dangerous. For one thing, as discussed in Chapter 5, it may shorten a woman's life. If you want as many years as possible with your wife, you don't want her underweight.

Furthermore, a superskinny woman may have — or be developing — an eating disorder. If so, no matter how attractive she is, think twice. You want a healthy wife, and eating disorders ravage physical and mental well-being. Anorexia can result in dry hair and skin, hair loss, a downy layer of hair (called lanugo) all over the body and face, fatigue and fainting, muscle deterioration and weakness, osteoporosis, and kidney and heart failure. Bulimia can lead to tooth decay and discoloration, gum disease, peptic ulcers, pancreatitis, gastric rupture (80% fatal), inflammation and rupture of the esophagus (which can cause circulatory collapse or death), and, like anorexia, heart failure. And both conditions are associated with listlessness, dullness, poor concentration, moodichaness, obsessive-compulsive disorder, anxiety, depression, and substance abuse.

Then there are other emotional issues. Do you want a wife suffering from low self-esteem and constantly demanding attention and approval? Can she raise emotionally and spiritually healthy children, or will she pass her own insecurities and dysfunctional eating on to them?

Finally, as one survivor puts it: "If you marry a woman with an eating disorder, you will be in a threesome: you, her, and her disease." After speaking with many men involved with such women, one writer sadly recounts: "These men spoke the words *bulimia* and *anorexia* as if they were the names of cruel and deviant men who had stolen their loves away. They looked so powerless during the telling of these stories, so abandoned." An eating disorder takes over a person's life. Such a person has limited emotional energy for anything else, including you.

Despite all these reasons to give an average-looking, medium-weight girl a try, you may worry what "the guys" will think if you wind up marrying her. If you believe a trophy wife makes you more of a man, you have some warped values and insecurities to work on (as many of us do). No one else has to see what you see in your spouse. Attraction can even be more compelling when it's private. A wife needn't boost your social stature, only your happiness.

Emotional articulacy, understanding, warmth, empathy, intelligence, humility, a love of life, a great sense of humor, kindness and compassion, generosity of spirit, idealism, creativity, confidence, authenticity — these things can make an ordinary-looking woman stunning.

Guys, the world is full of more beautiful women than you know. Don't pass up the one meant for you. Give real beauty a chance.

Conclusion

Love is the strongest force in the world. Real feminine beauty, combining outer and inner, probably runs a close second in its ability to move and motivate men. Tragically, society has corrupted these forces, giving rise to shallow physical gratification and self-display, and robbing love and beauty of their true power.

But ultimately, Judaism tells us, we will reclaim it. Long ago, Jewish mysticism promised that the final *tikkun* (rectification) of our world would come about through the harnessing of two tremendous strengths: transcending physicality and seeking essence. This means seeing beyond externals and connecting to what's internal, and resisting the seductiveness of superficial physicality and creating real relationships.*

* These powers are identified with the Biblical Rachel and her son Joseph, as described in the Chassidic work *Tiferet Shlomo* by Rabbi Shlomo HaKohen Rabinovich of Radomsk, *parashat Vayishlach*.

Using these strengths has been the subject of this book. When we transcend physicality and seek essence — and being *shomer negiah* plays no small part in both — we can build deep relationships. This ability is rooted in *tzniut*, which allows us to identify ourselves and others as the precious souls we are.

We can all help humanity move closer to its ideal. We can redeem our relationships, our bodies, and the holiness within us — and fix our world — by choosing to love.

Notes

Preface

page

10 "*We teach what we need to learn...need to know*": Steinem, *Revolution from Within*, 6.

Introduction

page

14 *"the life of the soul...human relationships"*: Gurian, *The Wonder of Girls*, 288.

Part One: Loving Another

page

18 *Healthy self-love is a prerequisite...everything you believe you aren't:* Brygel, "Swamped with Singles."

Chapter 1: The Real Thing

page

23 *"Love is a verb"*: Covey, *The Seven Habits of Highly Effective People*, 79–80.

23 *In expressing care, respect...we create love:* See Fromm, *The Art of Loving*, and Dessler, *Michtav Me'Eliyahu*.

24 *Love is the emotional attachment...another's goodness:* Based on the teachings of Rabbi Noach Weinberg (of blessed memory), founder of Yeshivat Aish HaTorah.

24 "*Love is not just feeling...lover and beloved*": Ginott, *Between Parent and Teenager*, 176.

29 *In romantic love you want...other person:* Adler, *She Said, She Said*, 125, citing Margaret Anderson.

30 *"engage in a full-blown idealization...blocked out reality:"* Wallerstein and Blakeslee, *The Good Marriage*, 47.

30 *"[This documented brain state]...thirst, and hunger":* Brizendine, *The Female Brain*, 66, citing A. Aron et al., "Reward, Motivation, and Emotion Systems Associated with Early-Stage Intense Romantic Love," *Journal of Neurophysiology* 94 (2005) (1): 327–37; D. M. Small et al., "Changes in Brain Activity Related to Eating Chocolate: From Pleasure to Aversion," *Brain* 124 (2001) (9): 1720–33; and D. Denton et al., "Neuroimaging of Genesis and Satiation of Thirst and an Interceptor-Driven Theory of Origins of Primary Consciousness," *Proceedings of the National Academy of Science USA* 96 (1999) (9): 5304–9.

30 *"The brain circuits that are activated...the next fix":* Ibid., 66, citing T. R. Insel and R. D. Fernald, "How the Brain Processes Social Information: Searching for the Social Brain," *Annual Review of Neuroscience* 27 (2004): 697–722.

30 *this overcharged brain state...a year or two:* Ibid., 69–70.

31 *Such a relationship involves...feelings of connection:* Ibid., 70–1.

33 *The idealization that's so dangerous...Mr. or Ms. Right:* See Wallerstein and Blakeslee, *The Good Marriage*, 48.

33 *Research has found that young...these images:* Kilbourne, *Can't Buy My Love*, 133, citing V. C. Strasburger, "Adolescent Sexuality and the Media," *Pediatric Clinics of North America* 36 (June 1989) (3): 747–73.

33 *married men shown photos...their marriages:* "Relationships," citing David M. Buss, *Evolutionary Psychology* (New York: Atlyn & Bacon, 1999), 154.

33 *another group of married men...their wives:* Shalit, *A Return to Modesty*, 53, citing James B. Allen et al., "Arousal and Attraction," *Journal of Personality and Social Psychology* 57 (1989) (2): 261–70; and Douglas T. Kenrick et al., "Influence of Popular Erotica on Judgments of Strangers and Mates," *Journal of Experimental Social Psychology* 25 (1989) (2): 159–67.

34 *From the 1930s, when mass media...in 1939:* "Relationships," citing David M. Buss, *Evolutionary Psychology* (New York: Atlyn & Bacon, 1999), 145.

35 *gazes back at her lovingly... "beautiful as ever":* Albom, *The Five People You Meet in Heaven*, 186–7.

37 *the conjoined twins Abigail and Brittany Hensel...and even drive:* "Abigail and Brittany Hensel." See also video clips at http://www.youtube.com.

38 *In mature love, each person...best self:* See Ginott, *Between Parent and Teenager*, 177.

39 *Decades earlier, Rabbi Wasserman's commitment...this world:* Personal communication with Rabbi Noach Orlowek, October 15, 2009.

40 *"God's greatest gift, after life itself...that he is":* Schlessinger, *The Proper Care and Feeding of Husbands*, 4.

Chapter 2: Creating the Space for Love

page

42 *Touch bonds — especially for women:* See Guéguen, "Courtship Compliance," 81–82, 86, 94–5, citing numerous studies; and Carey, "Evidence That Little Touches Do Mean So Much."

42 *Without the illusion of emotional closeness...genuine worth:* See Gurian, *The Wonder of Girls*, 262.

44 *When a woman gives birth...her newborn:* Brizendine, *The Female Brain*, 101–102.

44 *When she nurses, waves of oxytocin...her baby:* Ibid., 106, citing Kerstin Uvnäs-Moberg, "Oxytocin May Mediate the Benefits of Positive Social Interaction and Emotion, *Psychoneuroendocrinology* 23 (November 1988) (8): 819–35; and Kerstin Uvnäs-Moberg, *The Oxytocin Factor* (New York: Perseus, 2003).

44 *When a man and woman are physically intimate...and committed:* Ibid., 82.

44 *Hugging will do it. ...just touch:* Ibid., 67–68, 71–72.

45 *It turns off skepticism. ...kiss your judgment goodbye:* Ibid., 68, citing K. C. Light et al., "More Frequent Partner Hugs and Higher Oxytocin Levels Are Linked to Lower Blood Pressure and Vascular Resistance during Stress in Post-Menopausal Women on Estrogen Replacement," *Hormonal Behavior* 47 (2005) (5): 540–8; and C. S. Carter, "Neuroendocrine Perpsectives on Social Attachment and Love," *Psychoneuroendocrinology* 23 (1998) (8): 779–818 (1998); Kuchinskas, *The Chemistry of Connection*, 86.

45 *a leading neuropsychiatrist's advice...trust him:* Brizendine, *The Female Brain*, 68.

45 *Estrogen, the "female" hormone...diminishes it:* Kuchinskas, *The Chemistry of Connection*, 18.

45 *"Girls should learn that bonding...one for me":* Ibid., 119.

45 *Most young teenage boys...bond with them:* Ibid., 121–2.

46 *boys and girls "have seriously"...comes to relationships:* Brizendine, *The Female Brain*, 39.

46 *"It is a girl's task...an object":* Ginott, *Between Parent and Teenager*, 169.

46 *married men have somewhat less...likely to marry:* Kuchinskas, *The Chemistry of Connection*, 103, citing P. B. Gray et al., "Social Variables Predict Between-Subject but Not Day-to-Day Variation in the Testosterone of U.S. Men," *Psychoneuroendrocinology* 29 (2004) (9): 1153–62.

47 *In a book instructing men...why he* is: Shalit, *Girls Gone Mild*, 201, citing Ron Louis and David Copeland, *How to Succeed*

with Women (New York: Reward, 1998), 206.

47 *With enough such experiences...sense of self:* See Gurian, *The Wonder of Girls*, 269.

47 *Most of those who suffer...are women:* Grossman, *Unprotected*, 4, citing A. Levine and J. Cureton, "What We Know about Today's College Students," *About Campus*, March–April 1998.

48 *men have up to 100 times...woman's brain:* Brizendine, *The Female Brain*, 89, 91.

48 *some definitely will lie...they want:* Ibid., 64, citing David M. Buss, "Psychological Sex Differences: Origins through Sexual Selection," *American Psychology* 50 (1995) (3): 164–8, discussion 169–71; and W. Tooke, "Patterns of Deception in Intersexual and Intrasexual Mating Strategies," *Ethology and Sociobiology* 12 (1991) (5): 345–64.

48 *Chemically, we humans — men and women...for monogamy:* Kuchinskas, *The Chemistry of Connection*, 2, citing T. R. Insel, "A Neurological Basis of Social Attachment," *American Journal of Psychiatry* 154 (1997) (6): 726–35; Ibid., 11, 18, 93.

48 *Ultimately, men want and need...soul mate:* National Marriage Project.

48 *"We are both, women and men...lonely planet":* Martin, *Perfect Girls, Starving Daughters*, 192.

50 *"Experience is a good teacher...terrific bills":* Adler, *She Said, She Said*, 34, citing Minna Antrim, *Naked Truth and Veiled Illusions* (1902).

50 *The part of the brain responsible ...they felt:* Gurian, *The Wonder of Girls*, 36, 61.

53 *Ideally, we learn to produce oxytocin...years of life:* Kuchinskas, *The Chemistry of Connection*, 21–2.

53 *Early emotional deprivation, therefore...no emotional bonding:* Ibid., "The Oxytocin Gap."

53 *the brain can grow and change...produce oxytocin:* Ibid., *The Chemistry of Connection*, 3, 45.

54 *Mothers don't use up...additional children:* Ibid., "The Oxytocin Gap."

54 *"Think of the oxytocin response...feeling bonded":* Ibid.

58 *gazing into someone's eyes...oxytocin response:* Brizendine, *The Female Brain*, 68, citing Kerstin Uvnäs-Moberg, *The Oxytocin Factor* (New York: Perseus, 2003), and Rebecca Anne Turner et al., "Preliminary Research on Plasma Oxytocin in Normal Cycling Women: Investigating Emotion and Interpersonal Distress," *Psychiatry* 62 (1999) (2): 97–113; Kuchinskas, *The Chemistry of Connection*, 143, citing Paul J. Zak, "Trust: A Temporary Human Attachment Facilitated by Oxytocin," *Behavioral and Brain Sciences* 28 (2005) (3): 368–9.

58 *One study found that when...are activated:* Brizendine, *The Female Brain*, 5, citing Steven W. Gangestad and Randy Thornhill, "Menstrual Cycle Variation in Women's Preferences for the Scent of Symmetrical Men," *Proceedings, Biological Sciences* 265 (1998) (1339): 927–33; and Deborah Tannen, "Gender Differences in Topical Coherence: Creating Involvement in Best Friends' Talk," *Discourse Processes: Special Gender and Conversational Interaction* 13 (1990) (1): 73–90. See also Guéguen, "The Effect of a Woman's Incidental Tactile Contact on Men's Later Behavior," 263, citing A. Abbey, "Misperceptions of Friendly Behavior as Sexual Interest: A Survey of Naturally Occurring Incidents," *Psychology of Women Quarterly* 11 (1987): 173–94.

Part Two: Loving Yourself

page

66 *Hence women's generally greater sensitivity...self-revelation:* See Shalit, *A Return to Modesty*, especially ch. 7.

Chapter 3: The Core Connection

page

69 *When author Wendy Shalit...he had sneezed:* Shalit, *A Return to Modesty*, 3.

71 Ohr, *leather, begins with the letter...darkened world:* Hacohen, "*Shiviti Hashem LeNegdi Tamid,*" 281.

72 *"veer off the track...know is right":* Goldin, *6 Diaries*, 117.

72 *The resulting self-image could be called...impressions of us:* Hess-Biber, *Am I Thin Enough Yet?*, 59, citing C. H. Cooley, *Social Organization* (New York: Schocken Books, 1962 [1909]).

72 *"I am who I think you think I am":* Personal communication with clinical sociologist Leah Schachter, October 13, 2009, citing sociologist Charles Horton Cooley.

74 *Listen to nineteen-year-old Laurie..."a trifle":* Alcott, *Little Women*, 326–7.

78 *"You can't just* do...***be*** tzniut*":* Goldin, *6 Diaries*, 191–2.

78 *"It's that small voice...*this isn't me!*":* Ibid., 149.

80 *"When underwear becomes outerwear...nature of intimacy":* Brumberg, *The Body Project*, 136.

81 *This belief traditionally prevented parents...safeguarding their childhood:* See Postman, *The Disappearance of Childhood.*

82 *"A society that has declared war...hostile to women:"* Shalit, *A Return to Modesty*, 39.

82 *The minute a girl..." their existence":* Levine, *Mystics, Mavericks, and Merrymakers*, 213–4.

82 *disturbing description of an eight-year-old..."so cute?":* Martin, *Perfect Girls, Starving Daughters*, 336.

83 *A young woman who spent time..."realm of [male-female relationships]":* Levine, *Mystics, Mavericks, and Merrymakers*, 214.

83 *"Children are the living messages...not see":* Postman, *The Disappearance of Childhood*, xi.

86 *a couple who consulted..."his glasses":* Thanks to Rabbi Mordechai Rhine of Cherry Hill, NJ for this story.

87 *She's your sister:* Thanks to an NCSY rabbi for this idea.

88 *"'Are there any hot girls...my soul'":* Martin, *Perfect Girls, Starving Daughters*, 181.

94 *When Chaya Sara was twenty..."good place":* See Rigler, *Holy Woman*, 19–20.

95 *"When I see my reflection...really am":* Goldin, *6 Diaries*, 35.

95 *A therapist who works..."'Who are you?'":* Pipher, *Reviving Ophelia*, 254.

95 *A doctor who counsels..."only forgotten":* Remen, *My Grandfather's Blessings*, 108.

95 *A young woman sick of...*"my soul?"*:* Martin, *Perfect Girls, Starving Daughters*, 293.

96 *A leading feminist urges..."shines from within":* Steinem, *Revolution from Within*, 225.

Chapter 4: Saying No to the Media

page

97 *Much more than males...inner qualities:* Frederickson, "That Swimsuit Becomes You."

98 *perfecting it has mushroomed...mission in life:* See Brumberg, *The Body Project*, 1997.

98 *In the U.S. alone...$250 billion annually:* "Advertising and the End of the World — A Summary."

98 *Already in 2000, the typical...23% less:* Tiggemann et al., "'I Would Rather Be Size 10 than Have Straight A's'."

98 *In 1999, a study...lose weight:* Field et al., "Exposure to the Mass Media and Weight Concerns among Girls."

99 *A* Glamour *survey found...on the job:* Wolf, *The Beauty Myth*, 185–6, citing Drs. Wayne and Susan Wooley, "33,000 Women Tell How They Really Feel about Their Bodies," *Glamour*, February 1984.

99 *Among the grade-schoolers...prone to diet:* Field et al., "Exposure to the Mass Media and Weight Concerns among Girls."

99 *college-age women exposed...their bodies:* Bessenoff, "Can the Media Affect Us?"

99 *Fijians long believed that big...rampant in Fiji:* Goode, "Study Finds TV Alters Fiji Girls' View of Body"; Ireland, "Fijian

Girls Succumb to Western Dysmorphia."

100 *A computer-generated model...die of malnutrition:* Gerber, "Beauty and Body Image in the Media."

100 *Advertising doesn't sell only products...success, and normalcy:* Kilbourne, *Can't Buy My Love*, 76.

100 *since this self is empty...fill ourselves up:* Ibid., 257–8.

101 *Puberty floods a girl's brain...her looks:* Brizendine, *The Female Brain*, 31.

101 *women are highly sensitive to social messages:* Maine, *Father Hunger*, 32.

101 *Even more than two decades ago...considered "plain":* Steinem, *Revolution from Within*, 228–29, citing Rita Freedman, *Bodylove: Learning to Like Our Looks — and Ourselves* (New York: Harper & Row, 1988), 21–5.

101 *"the core belief of American culture"...even re-created:* Kilbourne, *Can't Buy My Love*, 223.

101 *"True beauty," the cosmetic industry tells us..."compacts, and tubes":* Personal communication with Leah Schachter, citing Laurence J. Peter, *Peter's Almanac* (New York: William Morrow & Co., 1982).

101 *"Why is it never said...*the body*?":* Wolf, *The Beauty Myth*, 66, paraphrasing Betty Friedan.

102 *Virtually no one can intelligently process...* "all *the time":* Martin, *Perfect Girls, Starving Daughters*, 147.

102 *advertising is our culture...cultural influence:* Kilbourne, *Can't Buy My Love*, 64, citing S. Jhally, *Advertising and the End of the World*, Media Education Foundation, video.

102 *Many males as well insist...imperfect one:* Martin, *Perfect Girls, Starving Daughters*, 176–77.

102 *"Back in 1915, only men...caught on":* See "Safety Razor Quiz."

103 *"Almost as soon as the phrase...clothes and boyfriends":* Lamb and Brown, *Packaging Girlhood*, 205.

103 *blurb from a children's Web site..."same time!":* Lamb and Brown, *Packaging Girlhood*, 245.

104 *"I think the power of* tzniut*...entire life":* Goldin, *6 Diaries*, 54.

105 *there's something genuinely attractive..."pin down":* Lamb and Brown, *Packaging Girlhood*, 287.

108 *"notorious incubator of the worst...fears and phobias":* Martin, *Perfect Girls, Starving Daughters*, 14.

108 *"a dominant and disturbing influence on the national psyche":* Pipher, *Reviving Ophelia*, 291.

108 *"Sometimes I sit on a subway car...like this":* Martin, *Perfect Girls, Starving Daughters*, 217.

110 *"Knowing what is real...first place":* Remen, *Kitchen Table Wisdom*, 77.

Chapter 5: Ending the Hunger for Selfhood

page

112 *Both anorexics and bulimics...father-child attachments:* Gurian, *The Wonder of Girls*, 110.

112 *the American Psychiatric Association...anorexia or bulimia:* Maine, *Father Hunger*, xiii, citing the American Psychiatric Association, "Practice Guidelines for the Treatment of Eating Disorders" (revision), *American Journal of Psychiatry*, 157 (January 2000) (1), Supplement, 1–39.

113 *"mental anorexics":* Wolf, *The Beauty Myth*, 183.

113 *are only a hairbreadth away from real illness:* Martin, *Perfect Girls, Starving Daughters*, 34.

113 *these cases may account...15% of adoloscents:* Natenshon, "Jews and Eating Disorders."

113 *Psychologists even measure...like yourself:* Brumberg, *The Body Project*, xxiv–v.

114 *A 1994 Diet Rite ad...retract the ad:* Bass, "Boycott Called on 'Anorexic' Ads."

114 *Tragically, emaciated females often receive...they're hospitalized:* Pipher, *Reviving Ophelia*, 175.

114 *Comparing Metropolitan Life's...gap for women:* Hess-Biber, *Am I Thin Enough Yet?*, 63.

114 *A popular girls' magazine...by a truck:* Martin, *Perfect Girls, Starving Daughters*, 1, citing E. Bothorol et al., "Love Your Body: Body Image Survey," *ELLEgirl*, February 2006.

114 *girls who worry they're fat...attempt suicide:* Ellin, "Dad, Do You Think I Look Too Fat?"

114 *girls and women are being seduced...salvation lies:* Hess-Biber, *Am I Thin Enough Yet?*, 10–11.

115 *"normative obsession":* Wolf, *The Beauty Myth*, 187, citing psychologist Judith Rodin.

115 *"imitative anorexia" or "imitative bulimia"...their bodies:* Hess-Biber, *Am I Thin Enough Yet?*, 82.

115 *"[Many] young women with eating disorders...matter of degree":* Pipher, *Reviving Ophelia*, 184.

115 *"culturally induced eating":* Hess-Biber, *Am I Thin Enough Yet?*, 82.

115 *"Our dissatisfaction is never, at it deepest, about our bodies":* Martin, *Perfect Girls, Starving Daughters*, 211.

115 *This is what Israeli super-model...and emptiness:* See Keret, *HaNashim HaYafot*.

115 *"harbor black holes at the center of [their] beings":* Martin, *Perfect Girls, Starving Daughters*, 6.

115 *Yael, an anorexic actress..."economic value":* Keret, *HaNashim HaYafot*, 89.

116 *Jane, a bulimic model..."good for me":* Ibid., 63.

116 *Avishag, a bulimic actress..."I have fat":* Ibid., 135.

116 *"Young women wage war...inner emptiness":* Maine, *Father Hunger*, xvi.

117 *one of the most successful treatments...sense of self:* Lamb and Brown, *Packaging Girlhood*, 186.

118 *Research in Israel has found...other girls:* "University of Haifa Study Shows a Connection between Religiosity and Body Self-Image."

118 *A similar study of Jewish women...eating disorders:* Peyser, *Body & Soul*, 16, citing M.E. Gluck and A. Geliebter, "Body Image and Eating Behaviors in Secular and Orthodox Jewish Women," *The Journal of Gender-Specific Medicine* 5 (2002) (1): 19–24.

118 *Observant girls who are typically...anyone else:* See Peyser, *Body & Soul,* 16, citing S. H. Kahn, "Hebrew Academy Targets Teenage Eating Disorders," *Cleveland Jewish News*, August 21, 1998, 24; and L. Pinhas et al., "Disordered Eating among Jewish Adolescent Females," unpublished abstract.

118 *one study conducted in a cosmopolitan area...general population:* Peyser, *Body & Soul,* 17, citing F. Kraft, "When Dieting Turns Deadly," *The Canadian Jewish News*, February 5, 1998.

118 *When she was twenty-seven..."trade places with anyone":* See Rosenblatt, *Finding Light in the Darkness.*

120 *Paternal support greatly boosts...emotional well-being:* Pipher, *Reviving Ophelia*, 118.

120 *"All love is unconditional...just approval":* Remen, *Kitchen Table Wisdom*, 47.

120 *a father's physical or (worse)..."father hunger":* See Maine, *Father Hunger*, especially chs. 7–8.

120 *there's no substitute for it:* Maine, *Father Hunger*, xv.

120 *"A father's love can make or break a girl":* Gurian, *The Wonder of Girls*, 156.

121 *"Relationships are what hold girls' lives in place":* Pipher, *Reviving Ophelia*, 189.

122 *"Girls' symptoms reflect the grief...true selves":* Pipher, *Reviving Ophelia*, 258.

Part Three: Getting There

Chapter 6: Building Love

page

126 *Research has shown virtually...wealth and happiness:* Herper, *"Money Won't Buy You Happiness."*

127 *invite anyone interested in you...getting to know:* "Relationships."

128 *One American graduate student...called it "brilliant": Inspired.*

130 *Not only does oxytocin...promotes healing:* Kuchinskas, *The Chemistry of Connection*, 1–3; Dobson, "How the Power of

Touch Reduces Pain and Even Fights Disease."

130 *Even altruism can release oxytocin...even a pet:* See Kuchinskas, *The Chemistry of Connection*, 19, 23, 55, and ch. 7; Ibid., "Recovering from MDMA Burnout."

130 *Even the smallest good deed..."helper's high":* "Is Atrusim Good for the Altrusitic Giver?"; Stossel and Johnson, "Doing Good, and Feeling Better."

130 *Loneliness can reflect a craving for oxytocin:* Kuchinskas, *The Chemistry of Connection*, 55.

132 *"I don't really understand...'my soul'?":* Goldin, *6 Diaries*, 32.

138 *Dr. Rahamim Melamed-Cohen..."years of my life":* See Rigler, *Lights from Jerusalem*, 417–31.

140 *One magazine cover featured...blended images:* Maine, *Father Hunger*, 42.

141 *"God, let me see [myself]...the world's":* Martin, *Perfect Girls, Starving Daughters*, 307.

142 *It's been found that religious involvement...mental well-being:* Grossman, *Unprotected*, 40, citing J. S. Levin and L. M. Chatters, "Research on Religion and Mental Health: An Overview of Empirical Findings and Theoretical Issues," Harold G. Koenig, ed., *Handbook of Religion and Mental Health* (San Diego: Academic Press, 1998), 33–50.

142 *prayer and other religious rituals...empowerment, and contentment:* Grossman, *Unprotected*, 41.

142 *Body dissatisfaction, where most eating disorders...their mothers:* Lowes and Tiggemann, "Body Dissatisfaction, Dieting Awareness and the Impact of Parental Influence in Young Children"; Maine, *Father Hunger*, 235.

143 *If you're a father...eating disorder:* Dixon et al., "Exploring Parental Influences on the Dieting Behavior of Adolescent Girls."

143 *Show her that you value substance in a woman:* Maine, *Father Hunger*, 50.

143 *One fifteen-year-old recalls...inner beauty:* Martin, *Perfect Girls, Starving Daughters*, 67.

143 *Don't use food to reward...at all ages:* Stanton, "Help Your Child Develop a Positive Body Image."

Final Words

page

152 *"the act of seeing can transform...our lives":* Remen, *My Grandfather's Blessings*, 93.

154 *Anorexia can result in dry hair...substance abuse:* "Health Consequences of Eating Disorders"; "General Information — Medical Complications from Eating Disorders."

155 *"These men spoke the words...so abandoned":* Martin, *Perfect Girls, Starving Daughters*, 192.

References

"Abigail and Brittany Hensel: An Extraordinary Bond." Mail Online, last updated December 13, 2006. http://www.dailymail.co.uk/femail/article-425736/Abigail-Brittany-Hensel-extraordinary-bond.html. Retrieved October 11, 2009.

Adler, Gloria, ed. *She Said, She Said: Strong Words from Strong-Minded Women.* New York: Avon Books, 1995.

"Advertising and the End of the World — A Summary." http://hope.journ.www.ed/tpilgrim/j190/adendofworldvidsum.html. Retrieved June 14, 2009.

Albom, Mitch. *The Five People You Meet in Heaven.* London: Time Warner Books, 2003. (Film directed by Lloyd Kramer, 2004.)

Alcott, Louisa May. *Little Women.* New York: Penguin Books, 1989 [1868].

Bass, Alison. "Boycott Called on 'Anorexic' Ads." *Boston Globe,* April 25, 1994, 16.

Bessenoff, Gayle. "Can the Media Affect Us? Social Comparison, Self-Discrepancy, and the Thin Ideal." *Psychology of Women Quarterly* 30 (2006): 239–51.

Brizendine, Louann, M.D. *The Female Brain.* New York: Morgan Books, 2006.

Brumberg, Joan Jacobs. *The Body Project: An Intimate History of American Girls*. New York: Vintage Books, 1997.

Brygel, Yael. "Swamped with Singles." *In Jerusalem* (*Jerusalem Post*), January 8, 2010.

Carey, Benedict. "Evidence That Little Touches Do Mean So Much." *New York Times*, February 23, 2010, D5.

Covey, Stephen. *The Seven Habits of Highly Effective People*. New York: Fireside/Simon & Schuster, 1989.

Dessler, Rabbi Eliyahu Eliezer (1963). *Michtav Me'Eliyahu*, vol. 1, "*Kuntras HaChesed*." B'nei Brak: Committee for the Publication of the Writings of Rabbi E. E. Dessler. [English: *Strive for Truth*. Jerusalem: Feldheim Publishers, 1978.]

Dixon, R. S., J. M. W. Gill, and V. A. Adair. "Exploring Paternal Influences on the Dieting Behaviors of Adolescent Girls." *Eating Disorders: The Journal of Treatment and Prevention* 11 (spring 2003) (1): 39–50.

Dobson, Roger. "How the Power of Touch Reduces Pain and Even Fights Disease." *The Independent*, October 10, 2006.

Ellin, Abby. "Dad, Do You Think I Look Too Fat?" *New York Times*, September 17, 2000.

Field, A. E., L. Cheung, A. M. Wolf, D. B. Herzog, S. L. Gortmaker, and G. A. Colditz. "Exposure to the Mass Media and Weight Concerns among Girls." *Pediatrics* 103 (March 1999) (3): 36–41.

Frederickson, Barbara L. "That Swimsuit Becomes You: Sex Differences in Self-Objectification, Restrained Eating, and Math Performance." *Journal of Personality and Social Psychology* 75 (1998) (1): 269–84.

Fromm, Erich. *The Art of Loving*. New York: Harper & Row, 1956.

"General Information — Medical Complications from Eating Disorders." Anorexia Nervosa and Associated Disorders. http://anad.org/22385/22406.html. Retrieved June 22, 2009.

Gerber, Robin. "Beauty and Body Image in the Media." Media Awareness Network, April 27, 2006. http://www.media-awareness.

ca/english/issues/stereotyping/womenandgirls/women_beauty.cfm. Retrieved December 6, 2009.

Ginott, Haim G. *Between Parent and Teenager*. New York: Avon Books, 1969.

Goldin, Aliza. *6 Diaries: Six Teens Take a New Look at Tznius*. Southfield, MI: Targum Press, 2009.

Goode, Erica. "Study Finds TV Alters Fiji Girls' View of Body." *New York Times*, May 20, 1999, A17.

Grossman, Miriam, M.D. *Unprotected: A Campus Psychiatrist Reveals How Political Correctness in Her Profession Endangers Every Student*. New York: Sentinel, 2007.

Guéguen, Nicolas. "Courtship Compliance: The Effect of Touch on Women's Behavior." *Social Influence* 2 (2007) (2): 81–97.

———. "The Effect of a Woman's Incidental Tactile Contact on Men's Later Behavior." *Social Behavior and Psychology* 38 (2010) (2): 257–66.

Gurian, Michael. *The Wonder of Girls: Understanding the Hidden Nature of Our Daughters*. New York: Atria Books, 2002.

Hacohen, Dina. "*Shiviti Hashem LeNegdi Tamid*" (I have set Hashem before me always). In *Kutnot Ohr* (Garments of light), edited by Ofir Schwartzbaum and Amichai Sadan. Jerusalem: Mechon 'Mofet' — Merkaz Hadrachah Pedagogi Torani, 2000.

"Health Consequences of Eating Disorders." National Eating Disorders Association. http://nationaleatingdisorders.org/p.asp?WebPage_ID=286&Profile_ID=41143. Retrieved June 22, 2009.

Herper, Matthew. "Money Won't Buy You Happiness." *Forbes*, September 21, 2004.

Hess-Biber, Sharlene. *Am I Thin Enough Yet? The Cult of Thinness and the Commercialization of Identity*. New York: Oxford University Press, 1996.

Inspired. Jewish Impact Films (Aish International). Video.

Ireland, Corydon. "Fijian Girls Succumb to Western Dysmorphia." Harvard University Gazette Online, March 12, 2009. http://

news.harvard.edu/gazette/?s=fijian+girls+succumb. Retrieved December 6, 2009.

"Is Altruism Good for the Altruistic Giver?" DUJS (Dartmouth Undergraduate Journal of Science) Online, spring 2009. http://dujs.dartmouth.edu/spring-2009/is-altruism-good-for-the-altruistic-giver. Retrieved November 30, 2009.

Johnson, Amanda K., Allyson Barnacz, Paul Constantino, Jason Triano, Todd K. Shackelford, and Julian Paul Keenan. "Female Deception Detection as a Function of Commitment and Self-Awareness." *Personality and Individual Differences* 37 (2004) (7): 1417–24.

Karremans, Johan C., Thijs Verwijmeren, Tila M. Pronk, and Reyke Reitsma. "Interacting with Women Can Impair Men's Cognitive Functioning." *Journal of Experimental and Social Psychology* 45 (July 2009) (4): 1141–4.

Kaufman, Scott Barry. "Interacting with Women Makes Men Stupid." *Psychology Today*, May 18, 2009.

Keret, Maayan. *HaNashim HaYafot* (The beautiful women). Tel Aviv: Miskal — Yediot Aharonot Books and Chemed Books, 2003.

Kilbourne, Jean. *Can't Buy My Love: How Advertising Changes the Way We Think and Feel.* New York: Touchstone, 1999.

Kuchinskas, Susan. *The Chemistry of Connection: How the Oxytocin Response Can Help You Find Trust, Intimacy, and Love.* Oakland: New Harbinger Publications, 2009.

———. "The Oxytocin Gap." August 14, 2009 post on http://hugthemonkey.com. Retrieved August 15, 2009.

———. "Recovering from MDMA Burnout." May 24, 2009 post on http://hugthemonkey.com. Retrieved August 20, 2009.

Lamb, Sharon, Ed.D., and Lyn Mikel Brown, Ed.D. *Packaging Girlhood: Rescuing Our Daughters from Marketers' Schemes.* New York: St. Martin's Griffin, 2006.

Levine, Stephanie Wellen. *Mystics, Mavericks, and Merrymakers: An Intimate Journey among Hasidic Girls.* New York: New York University Press, 2003.

Lowes, J. and M. Tiggemann. "Body Dissatisfaction, Dieting Awareness and the Impact of Parental Influence in Young Children." *The British Journal of Health Psychology* 8 (2003) (pt. 2): 135–47.

Maine, Dr. Margo. *Father Hunger: Fathers, Daughters, and the Pursuit of Thinness*. Carlsbad, CA: Gurze Books, 2004.

Mander, Jerry. *Four Arguments for the Elimination of Television*. New York: Morrow Quill Paperbacks, 1978.

Manolson, Gila. *Head to Heart: What to Know before Dating and Marriage*. Southfield, MI: Targum Press, 2002.

———. *The Magic Touch: A Jewish Approach to Relationships* (revised and expanded edition). Southfield, MI: Targum Press, 1999.

———. *Outside/Inside: A Fresh Look at Tzniut* (revised and expanded edition). Southfield, MI: Targum Press, 2005.

Martin, Courtney E. *Perfect Girls, Starving Daughters: How the Quest for Perfection Is Harming Young Women*. New York: The Berkley Publishing Group, 2007.

Natenshon, Abigail, M.A., L.C.S.W., G.C.F.P. "Jews and Eating Disorders." www.eating-disorder-information.com/ed/jews. Retrieved August 13, 2009.

National Marriage Project. "Who Wants to Marry a Soul Mate? New Survey Findings on Young Adults' Attitudes about Love and Marriage." *The State of Our Unions*, 2001. http://marriage-rutgers.edu. Retrieved August 18, 2009.

Peyser, Dr. Caroline and ATID Fellows Research Team. *Body & Soul: A Guide for Addressing Eating Disorders in a Jewish Education Setting*. Jerusalem: Academy for Torah Initiatives and Directions, 2005.

Pipher, Mary, Ph.D. *Reviving Ophelia: Saving the Selves of Adolescent Girls*. New York: Ballantine Books, 1994.

Postman, Neil. *The Disappearance of Childhood*. New York: Vintage Books, 1994 [1982].

"Relationships." http://en.wikibooks.org/wiki/Relationships. Retrieved August 17, 2009.

Remen, Rachel Naomi, M.D. *Kitchen Table Wisdom: Stories That*

Heal. New York: Riverhead Books, 1996.

———. *My Grandfather's Blessings: Stories of Strength, Refuge, and Belonging.* New York: Riverhead Books, 2000.

Rigler, Sara Yoheved. *Holy Woman: The Road to Greatness of Rebbetzin Chaya Sara Kramer.* New York: Shaar Press, 2006.

———. *Lights from Jerusalem: Stories and Perspectives from the Holy City.* New York: Shaar Press, 2007.

Rosenblatt, Shaul. *Finding Light in the Darkness: The Toughest Challenges and How to Grow from Them.* Southfield, MI: Targum Press, 2006.

"Safety Razor Quiz: Gillette Early Years." http://www.safetyrazors.net/gillettequiz1.htm. Retrieved September 1, 2009.

Schlessinger, Dr. Laura. *The Proper Care and Feeding of Husbands.* New York: Harper, 2004.

Shalit, Wendy. *A Return to Modesty: Discovering the Lost Virtue.* New York: The Free Press, 1999.

———. *Girls Gone Mild: Young Women Reclaim Self-Respect and Find It's Not Bad to Be Good.* New York: Random House, 2007. (Republished as *The Good Girl Revolution: Young Rebels with Self-Esteem and High Standards.* New York: Ballantine, 2008.)

Stanton, Melissa. "Help Your Child Develop a Postive Body Image." *Baltimore's Child*, December 2009.

Steinem, Gloria. *Revolution from Within: A Book of Self-Esteem.* New York: Little, Brown & Company, 1992.

Stossel, John, and Sylvia Johnson. "Doing Good, and Feeling Better: Why Giving Back Could Make You Happier...and Healthier." ABC News, August. 20, 2007. http:// www.abcnews. go.com/2020/story?id=2685717. Retrieved November 30, 2009.

Tiggemann, M., M. Gardiner, and A. S. Slater. "'I Would Rather Be Size 10 than Have Straight A's': A Focus Study of Adolescent Girls' Wish to Be Thinner." *Journal of Adolescence* 23 (2000) (6): 645–59.

"University of Haifa Study Shows Connection between a Girl's

Religiosity and Body Self-Image." *The University in the Media*, April 6, 2006.

Wallerstein, Judith S., and Sandra Blakeslee. *The Good Marriage: How and Why Love Lasts*. New York: Warner Books, 1995.

Wolf, Naomi. *The Beauty Myth: How Images of Beauty Are Used against Women*. New York: Harper Perennial, 1991.

About the Author

Gila Manolson (née Marilyn Fisch) grew up in the northeastern United States and graduated magna cum laude from Yale University with a degree in music. In Israel, she studied at Neve Yerushalayim College for Women and elsewhere, most recently at Nishmat — the Jerusalem Center for Advanced Jewish Studies for Women. For five years, she was the resident supervisor of the women's Heritage House, a Jewish youth hostel in Jerusalem's Old City. A popular lecturer in numerous programs, schools, and seminaries in Israel, she teaches regularly at She'arim College of Studies for Jewish Women. Her overseas lecture tours have taken her to the U.S., Canada, Switzerland, South Africa, Russia, Argentina, and Chile. She is the author of *The Magic Touch: A Jewish Approach to Relationships*, *Outside/Inside: A Fresh Look at Tzniut*, and *Head to Heart: What to Know before Dating and Marriage*, which have been translated into several languages. She and her family live in Jerusalem.